D1379424

APPLETON–CENTURY PHILOSOPHY SOURCE-BOOKS

STERLING P. LAMPRECHT, *Editor*

CONCERNING THE TEACHER

AND

ON THE IMMORTALITY OF THE SOUL

UNIFORM WITH THIS VOLUME

St. Thomas Aquinas, *Concerning Being and Essence,* translated with the addition of a preface by George G. Leckie.

John Locke, *Treatise of Civil Government* and *A Letter Concerning Toleration,* edited by Charles L. Sherman.

Benedict de Spinoza, *Writings on Political Philosophy,* edited by A. G. A. Balz.

Immanuel Kant, *The Fundamental Principles of the Metaphysic of Ethics,* translated with an introduction by Otto Manthey-Zorn.

CONCERNING THE TEACHER
(De magistro)

and

ON THE IMMORTALITY OF THE SOUL
(De immortalitate animae)

BY

ST. AURELIUS AUGUSTINE
BISHOP OF HIPPO

"Fides quaerit, intellectus invenit."
De Trinitate, Bk. XV, Ch. 2.

Translated from the Latin with
the Addition of a Preface by

GEORGE G. LECKIE

Associate Professor of Philosophy
Elmira College

D. APPLETON–CENTURY COMPANY
INCORPORATED

New York   *London*

COPYRIGHT, 1938, BY

D. APPLETON–CENTURY COMPANY, INC.

*All rights reserved. This book, or parts
thereof, must not be reproduced in any
form without permission of the publisher.*

318

PRINTED IN THE UNITED STATES OF AMERICA

CONTENTS

PREFACE

In the writings of St. Augustine Greek and Roman ideas are endued with a fresh energy and truth through being made the instruments of a renewed vision. Viewed in retrospect, the task of St. Augustine was that of adjusting two cultural perspectives to each other in order to evolve a translated and unified *tertium comparationis*. This task he accomplished by joining Platonic cosmology, with its eternal realm of essences imitated imperfectly by the shadowy things of the temporal world, to the epic of the Judeo-Christian world with its dramatic account of the origin, fall, and redemption of man.

Tradition is the flowing stream of racial and cultural heritages on which all wise men must learn to navigate. In St. Augustine's thought there was not one tradition, habitual and unquestioned; rather, several traditions met in him, became confluent, and were commingled. By bringing Greek wisdom to perfection in Christian charity, he transformed one culture into another in such a way that both were strengthened in a more inclusive and sharper focus. This transfiguration contained a cultural patrimony which was to sustain and to nourish the speculations of subsequent centuries. In the *Confessions* is delineated one man's pilgrimage towards beatitude, but in *The City of God* the pilgrimage is raised to a procession of mankind through all ages along the road of eternal order. Because St. Augustine thought of history in terms of the emergence of error and its rectification by grace, he reduced historical episodes to a series of orderly mundane and cosmic transitions, thereby enlarging to universal proportions the route of his personal conversion as mediated by Platonic thought and Pauline motives.

Some books have the attribute of permanence, a certain magnitude of inexhaustible diversity in unity. Such books are suited to feed the imaginative sentiments and to quicken simultaneously the intellectual virtues of man. Applied to St. Augustine, this says that his works are classics, and it carries the extra suggestion that he was a poet. "But poets, or those who imagine and express this indestructible order, are not only the authors of language and music, of the dance and architecture, and statuary, and painting: they are the institutors of law, and the founders of civil society, and the inventors of the arts of life, and the teachers, who draw into a certain propinquity with the beautiful and the true, that partial apprehension of the agencies of the invisible world which is called religion. Hence all original religions are allegorical. . . ." [1]

Besides his poetic genius, St. Augustine possessed the discipline of a Latin rhetorician, by virtue of which the poet could become articulate, resourceful and universal. The universal is a property which makes a corpus of thought alive and cogent in any age. A renewal of creative energy requires vivid sentiments and a keen zest for action, but to survive the local signs of a specific occasion it requires also the extra dimension of intellectual formulation.

St. Augustine's intellectual curiosity seems to have been awakened by the Manichæans and their concrete myth-making propensity, to which was added a certain mystic tension. Later, under the caustic of the New Academy,[2] he underwent a thorough sceptical purging. But it was the leaven of Platonism,

---

[1] "A Defence of Poetry," p. 5, *Essays and Letters,* by Percy Bysshe Shelley, Camelot Classics, London, 1887.

[2] Cf. philosophical works of Cicero.

and more especially of Neoplatonism, that liberated him from sensualism and supplied him with a basis from which he was able to alleviate his scepticism. His writings indicate a subtle grasp of the function of an initial doubt, not only as a critical moment in the dialectic of truth but as an agent for cleansing the mind of an excess of empirical fancy.[3]

Platonism has often been cited as the bridge to Christian conversion, and certainly a Platonizing tendency guided St. Augustine through the progressive levels of recognition, reversal, and redirection involved in the metaphysics of conversion.[4] After St. Augustine's Platonic conversion the rhetorical eloquence of Ambrose, Bishop of Milan,[5] brought him into convergence with the urgency of St. Paul, and he passed beyond the foreshortened certitude of pagan philosophers. After a period of acute self-examination he found himself prepared for baptism.

His baptism carried with it the speculative and practical responsibilities of the Christian faith, and these responsibilities were met in one controversial emergency after another. His mastery of rhetorical formulation and the increase in ordered insight which accrued from the dialectical stages of his Platonizing tendency were to be powerful adjuncts in lifting him above the diversity of incidental events to the stable focus of a nontemporal point of view. St. Augustine was able to transform a rhetoric adapted to routine usage as a public instrument of panegyric and forensic into a rhetoric disciplined and clarified by metaphysical investigation. For this reason, in addition to the content of his doctrinal bequest, he should properly be called the true father of the scholastic tradition which reached its maturity in the thirteenth century.

[3] Cf. St. Augustine, *Contra academicos, Soliloquies.*
[4] Cf. St. Augustine, *De beata vita* and *De ordine.*
[5] Cf. St. Augustine, *The Confessions,* Bk. V, Ch. 13, *et seq.*

I

GENERAL IMPORT OF AUGUSTINIAN RHETORIC [6]

In his *De doctrina christiana,* wherein he formulated certain
rules of interpretation in regard to the Testaments, St. Augustine
dismissed the corrupt Roman sophistic of personal opportunism.
By way of reform he urged a return to the Greek ideal of
moving men to truth, an ideal so long truncated by the Roman
zeal for routine utility and practical prudence. Dignity of
thought and motives of great urgency, he advises, must replace
the frivolous Roman passion for literary style for the sake of
literary style, oratorical eloquence for the sake of verbal elegance, art for the sake of art. Henceforth art must be a means
of distributing the fund of revealed truth contained in the
Scriptures. Art, then, must be a catholic utility of the complete
man.

It has been said that St. Augustine not only possessed the
synthetic powers of poetic intuition, but that joined in the same
mind was the skill of a Latin rhetorician. It was this skill, re-
oriented by the Greek metaphysics of being, which enabled him
to formulate Christian doctrine and simultaneously to communi-
cate the poetic inspiration of the Scriptures to a Latinized people. St. Augustine belonged to the Western Empire, the civic
symbol of which was Rome; and the Latin Empire was the
imperium of the Latin language. Through this Latin rhetorician
imbued with the theology of grace, *rhetoric,* rather than being
a means to idle amusement or civic advancement, became an
instrument of discovery and disciplined inquiry. The reformed

[6] This is in no way intended as a factual or syntactic analysis of rhetoric.
For analysis of syntax see, e. g., *De la latinité des sermons de Saint Augustin,* par Ad. Regnier, Librairie Hachette et Cie., Paris, 1886.

professor of Latin eloquence sought no longer merely to delight and move, but rather indeed to provoke in men a scrutiny of their interior formal acts. Hence he led men to inquire and to teach themselves through themselves. He was providing for multiple agents of intelligence who would energize and distribute the deposit of faith, and he understood his function.

There were three classical ends of rhetoric treated by Cicero, codified by Quintilian, and possessed by St. Augustine, namely, *docere,* to instruct, *movere,* to move, *delectare,* to amuse and delight. Of these *docere* became the primary means to the end of truth which St. Augustine advanced. *Docere* employs signs and things signated to lead the mind from sensible things and images which are similitudes of such things to the education of ideas which are interior reflexive acts of man.[7] *Movere* is em-

---

[7] Signs: (1) *Natural*—preformed things of physical nature. These are multi-referential as elements in a complex analogically ordered world system. Preformed signs are intrinsic to the substances in the order of divine creation as it operates in the intricate network of material and changeable things. (2) *Cognitive* or *formal*—a formal act of cognition by virtue of which *that which* is signified (the signifiable) is signified. These interior formal acts or signs in cognition exist and signify in and through a formal (or analytically determinate) act of cognition. Thus a sign of this sort is a formal act or regulated habit of signifying the thing which is signified. There is in general a double origin of cognitive signs: natural preformed things exterior to the senses, and reflexive acts of thought. (3) *Conventional*—imposed by convention as, e. g., written marks or notations, audible syllables, mimetic patterns or gestures, and also parts of discourse: nouns, adjectives, verbs, etc. A conventional sign does not stand for a natural thing signified, but for a kind or sort of notation and its definition; a conventional sign has no real reference except through the medium of cognitive acts or signs. Hence conventional signs are partially based on arbitrary association, which is not true of cognitive signs which simulate the natures of things.

Cognitive and conventional signs are products of voluntary rational operations or distinctions: (a) cognitive signs as impositions or intentions, that is, as formal acts of understanding in conjunction with things sensed, images and reflexive acts of thought; (b) conventional signs as notational factors, just as, e. g., in the science of grammar: spelling, punctuation, or parsing of parts of speech in a secondarily imposed language, etc.

ployed in an auxiliary capacity to arouse in the poetic creature, who is animal as well as rational, a love of the interior act which moves from images in order to reveal ideas, or, ideas having been educed, to urge to action guided by such principles. *Delectare,* which during the inverted order of the second and third century A. D. sophistic had been the engrossing object of the language arts as expressed in personal or exterior display and literary virtuosity, sinks back into an incidental function.

Correctly conceived, of course, *delectare* is concerned with the joy which accrues from interior acts of contemplation associated with the evocation of ideas. The intellectual moment of discovery carries its own interior ecstasy and its own intrinsic rewarding gifts. In so doing, however, it refers beyond itself to a further luminous source in comparison with which even the light of its clearest moments is obscure indeed. As the mind moves from things to images and from images to ideas *delectare* is absorbed into the function *movere.* Thus delight no longer depends on the movement of exterior things, since it is made to issue from the very interior motion of thought. This conception of reformed *delectare* is capable of modifying profoundly the materials and formulations of art. It suggests, moreover, that there is a proper ratio or order of arts to each other.

When *delectare* is no longer trained by urgency of truth and liberal reflection, it tends towards mere ornamentation or incidental description. Hence the "unique," the curious or the singular, or perhaps merely the literal eventfulness of superficial events, come to occupy minute scrutiny and tireless elaboration. Cogency and dimensions of significance are sacrificed to variety. Associated with this, verbal eccentricity or elegance may be offered in place of depth of conception. Perhaps we may recall the Platonic strictures in the *Republic* against the sort of artists who at their best only give an imitation of an imitation in sensible fancies, and at their worst hold up such caricatures of reality as criteria and norms of perfection. The Aristotelian indictment cuts deeper than the Platonic, but for both Plato and Aristotle the dictum that art is the end of art would have been objectionable as the dissipation, perverse and unnatural, of functions which serve other ends.

When *delectare* is brought under *movere* in the interior sense and *movere* in turn is ordered under *docere,* all three modes become instruments of cogency. Cogency presupposes a message of great dignity touching upon man's most intimate concerns, perduring in its implications for man as man. In formulating Christian doctrine and in acting as its mediator to both the literate and illiterate, St. Augustine was to direct the arts once more towards their Greek ideal as instruments of truth. This redirection clearly entailed a reformation of the arts, and of these most especially the language arts which are essentially implicated with the interior formal acts of cognition by which men understand and are illuminated.

It has been suggested that St. Augustine should be conceived as a poet, but as a rhetorical-dialectical poet with the responsibilities of man's salvation energizing his sentiments and thoughts. The speculative and imaginative centers of energy active in the Græco-Roman and Judeo-Christian traditions fermenting in the stages of his personal conversion fused his thought into a poetic which moves through a connected series of analogies reflecting man's relation to God. Not only did he arrange and order the basic analogies, but within the terms of these analogies he ordered lesser analogies, thereby increasing simultaneously both the extensity and intensity of his vision. The ordering ideas of being, truth, unity, and goodness run through his networks of allegory, introducing a proper coördination of parts to parts and wholes to wholes with the generative point of projection from God's Unity and Being. In this historico-allegorical sort of dialectic, critical events and episodes are made to move in conformity with ideas which weave significance into factual diversity.

This sort of allegorizing is not without discipline. Rhetoric in the wide sense [8] is the art and discipline of allegory; for similitudes are not only concrete images but also something much more sophisticated, namely, complex constructions of the intellect. Such allegorical systems deal with the problematical, and they are matrices from which propositions are excised for syllogistic ordering. In order to gain an understanding of the function of St. Augustine as a rhetorical poet some general distinctions must first be formulated and clarified. Because the ratio of analogical induction to syllogistic deduction easily becomes obscured or lost where specialization intervenes, the 'Aristotelian' disruption of 'Platonic' allegories into syllogistic orders has long been subject to false polemic and mistaken affection. Hence we need to make a brief survey of poetic to see how this ratio is preserved and through what means.

Poetic (*poesis:* "making") in its classical setting is a mode of composition which moves from one simple or complex image or similitude to another according to an order of transitive sentiment. Its function is to feed the sentiments and to stimulate wit which is a gift for analogies; its end is to delight the mind by a movement of images in such a way as to provoke human concern. We are reminded of Jung's theory that phantasy arouses preformed images from slumber, and that these images create a psychic disturbance. The function of prose (argument), on the other hand, is to present ideas leading to some mode of explicated truth. Hence prose moves through ideas to ideas and in ideas it ends. Poetic approaches prose by suggesting ideas through images; prose approaches poetic by using images as examples, illustrations and instances. Thus, for purposes of discursive clarity, poetic is the contrary of prose, and prose is the

[8] Rhetoric in the stricter sense is discussed in Section III of this Preface.

contrary of poetic, but poetic and prose are coexistent contraries and not exclusive opposites. Consequently, poetic may overlap prose and prose may overlap poetic. In fact, in a nicely balanced case, one and the same composition might be read in one reference as poetic and in another as prose, while any piece of composition is apt to fluctuate up and down between the extremes.[9]

Poetic seems most alive when it is under the tug of the mystic, the hidden meaning or extra-increment of truth which eludes analysis. There is of course an intellectual discipline for mysticism, which is ordered by the anagogic movement intrinsic to the arts. It is possible to think of communication as oscillating between extreme poetic imagery on the one hand and extreme argumentative prose on the other. At the extreme of operational formalism, however, lies sterility unless reflection coöperates with wit to furnish analogical variations or a proper concrete diversity.

Both poetic and prose employ the arts of grammar, rhetoric, and logic as instruments of formulation. The intuitive mode or art of grammar names things. The art of rhetoric moves from one named image to another, collecting dispersed metaphors into related similes and fragmented similes into complex analogies, signifying one particular thing by another. The art of logic determines the relations between metaphors in similes and between the terms in analogies, and it generalizes these into modes of order. Grammar gives the initial names to things which are appropriated as metaphors by rhetoric. Rhetoric, dealing with antithesis, determines by opposites; illustrates by adducing analogies; exemplifies by showing instances; describes by applying unique features; enumerates by multiplying instances; draws parallels by constructing complex analogies; ex-

[9] Examples: *City of God* (poetic), *On the Trinity* (poetic-prose), *On the Immortality of the Soul* (prose).

pands by characterizing or relating to other terms. Logic abstracts the order, ratios, proportions, or relationships implicitly present in rhetorical patterns and reflexively knows these as they are in themselves. Analogy preserves a generality of form in altered matters of fact, so that, consequently, a concrete analogical medium is to rhetoric as an abstract relational schema is to logic. The task of logic is to explicate signs into a network of forms, that of rhetoric to *pre*form the material by assembling signs into analogies as potential for logical analysis. In addition to a gift of wit the mind requires the sophistication of discipline or a sure capacity for dealing with the simple and multi-directional implications of formal acts of cognition. There is a more subtle moment of this sort of analysis in which rhetoric turns on the terms of grammar and elaborates the simple terms which precede predicative modes. We shall return to this in the last section of this Preface. Poetry is the fecundity of vision; rhetoric the discipline of economy and preservation through formal elaboration and provisional order.

In the writings of St. Augustine rhetoric is an intermediary mode of formulation moving towards dialectical logic, the poetic moment moving towards a more luminous prose. But the movement is halted by an excess of diversity not yet properly assimilated through ideas. The fecundity of St. Augustine, however, lies in his analogy-making power by means of which he brings the less significant under the more significant. Without this intricating and ordering power it is inconceivable that he could have gathered so many floating threads of thought within the meshes of his doctrine. The critique of signs and signation, the investigation of the sort of confusions which symbols create, has already been given a certain degree of causal prefiguration in St. Augustine's speculations. The beginning of the scholastic attention to dialectic and the gradual subordination of grammar and rhetoric to the governing ideas of dialectic may be seen in an emergent state in the writings of St. Augustine. The *De ordine,* the *De magistro* and the *De musica,* for example, are rational seeds from which will come to flourish the intricately ramified tree of dialectical *Summae* which mature around the thirteenth century. And this tree is a tree of life, since the language arts are rational instruments promoting the health of the mind just as the natural instruments of the physician coöperate with nature to promote the health of the body.

II

GENERAL FEATURES OF ETHICAL DOCTRINE

St. Augustine's rhetorical skill placed him in an intermediary position between Greek speculation and the Testaments. The strategic center of doctrine turned about God's evocation of creatures from non-being and the message of transfiguration interfused in the Pauline Epistles. To understand St. Augustine's doctrine it is necessary to approach it through his central perspective, namely, that of the good.

Man's true dignity resides in his reason and the intentions of his will in so far as reason and will coöperate to render an enlightened service to God. Left to his own defective will which has been vitiated by Adam's original error, man has no plenary power through virtue of which he can work out his own salvation and create a perfected nature through his curtailed will. For Adam it was *posse non peccare,* but not *non posse peccare.* Adam did turn from God, and since this original defection the history of his descendants has been endlessly complicated by wayfaring incidents. For man, whose perfection is partially a function of his will, the activity towards the assimilation of perfection requires a second gift of nature in the form of grace over and beyond God's first gift of creation. Christ, the

Physician of the Soul, is the intermediary agent of redemption. Only by and through God's remedial gift of grace can man exceed himself and restore in himself the will to adhere to the order of love which originates from God and terminates in God. The contemplation of truth is a necessary condition for beatitude, but it is not a sufficient condition. Truth, as expressed in the Law of the Old Testament, is the formal condition of knowing the good, but in addition the will made healthy through grace must act as an efficient cause in order to transfer truth into action. St. Augustine does not repudiate the juridical function of truth, but he does insist that in its purely formal and routine aspect it is insufficient. Man must not only know truth, but he must also have the power to love its origin and thus loving its origin to abide by it.[10]

How shall man to whom grace has been given by Christ, the Physician of the Soul, appropriate that grace? This requires a certain amount of doctrinal clarification. There is an optimism in St. Augustine which has been distorted by later exploitations of his thought. The essence of Augustinian optimism is grounded in the condition that God's gift of remedial grace allows man's imperfections to be once more relatively perfectible. Both will and understanding are relatively perfectible, and each is implicated with and so involves the other. Man's will has been vitiated by Adam's error, but the grace of Christ works efficiently and formally in each man. An assigned capacity for good or evil, truth or falsehood, resides in the human animal. But truth and good require a self-developed discipline, if truth is to be made explicit and the good intelligible in the order of practical action. Through the intellectual virtues which consist in the mastery of the art of right thinking, man prepares himself for a lucid understanding of the moral virtues. Man is able to know the order of the good by virtue of his rational attribute.

[10] Cf. *On the Spirit and the Letter; On Nature and Grace; Enchiridion.*

Everything depends upon the decision which he will make or
not make to further in himself the illumination of God's image
which is situated in the interior man.

Through his doctrine of the Physician of Grace, St. Augustine of course teaches that God operates in the rituals and
sacraments. In ritualistic and sacramental routines the affirma-
tion of the interior acts of faith, hope, and charity support and
complete the pagan virtues of temperance, fortitude, prudence,
and justice. Thus the will is turned towards God as the origin
of beatitude. The routines of religion are, therefore, acts and
signs by which man is reminded of God. They awaken and
quicken in the mind the love of God and thus prepare the mind
to receive grace effectively.

St. Augustine's formula that faith inquires, but reason discovers and confirms, contains the figuration of disciplines essential to man's nature. The arts, moveover, and especially the
liberal disciplines, are speculative analogues of the sacraments
which are exterior signs of an interior grace. Faith is an act of
belief and prepares the mind for inquiry, but reason investigates
the intelligibility of that which is believed. The function of
faith (or the will to believe, love, and inquire) is contained
under the analogy of Christ as the Physician of the Soul, but the
function of reason (or the power to reflect and understand) is
contained under the analogy of Christ as the Interior Master or
teacher operative in man's essential nature which is reason. The
question of how man knows and the origin of truth is the
permanent center of Augustinian speculation.

St. Augustine's treatise *On the Trinity* gives a nice focal picture of the problem. This treatise has a beginning, a middle, and
an end by means of which inquiry reaches its object through
an ordered series of analogies. It begins with the Godhead and
the triune relationships of the Trinity, three relatively and one
substantially. The middle explains man's nature as a recipient

of grace, and the end man's relation to God through Christ. From the formulation of the Trinity, St. Augustine takes the master relationships which govern the multiple and copious features of his subordinate analogies.[11]

At the inception of the middle scene,[12] man's efficient contact with sensible natures is elaborated. Sensation and sensible memory, with the acts of attention involved, are functions of the *exterior man* by means of which he is contingent to the preformed signs or corporeal things of material and temporal nature as a whole. Corporeal natures, created by God, are instrumental and symbolic. But the process of sensation and sensible memory is such that the symbolic and vestigial features of natural things are obscurely veiled. Sensible memory retains in a latent state a vast deposit of confused and dispersed metaphors of nature. These require piecing together, so that they are reintegrated into complex patterns or analogical similitudes of nature. As thus formulated the complex formulæ reveal synoptically the *speculum Dei* which exists in the material and temporal dimensions of the world. The constructive function of science is that of generically exploring and integrating the confused metaphors of sensible memory. This formal task requires the intervention of liberal disciplines, and in this respect it is evident that St. Augustine is reëxpressing the Platonic program for the Academy.[13]

---

[11] Cf. *On the Trinity*, Bks. I–VIII.

[12] Cf. *On the Trinity*, Bks. VIII–XV.

[13] Cf. Plato, *The Republic*, Bks. VI–VIII. Prior to his treatise *On the Trinity*, St. Augustine had long since undergone the purge of initial doubt and established that man may know three things about himself with certitude: (1) that he is, (2) that he lives, (3) that he knows or possesses truth as an attribute of his thinking substance. The argument in the *Soliloquies*, Bk. II, Chs. 11–15, modeled on the Platonic *Phaedo* to the effect that truth abides in the soul as in a subject, that truth cannot perish, hence, so much less can the soul perish, is reformulated in *On the Immortality of the Soul*. The subjacent argument of the *Phaedo* based on the figure of the soul as a harmony of the body (*Soliloquies*, Bk. II, Chs. 14, 18, 19) is profoundly modified in

The discovery of the confused signs of the sensed world in sensible memory leads to the recognition and distinction of a further dimension of understanding, namely, that of intellect.[14] On this level of the *inner man,* thought reflecting on itself and knowing itself knows in this formal unity of cognition an aspect of truth not revealed as such in the diversity of sensed information. The formal power of that which understands and that by virtue of which it understands must be prior to that which is understandable. At this intersection a very important condition enters. *No sign can be said to be known perfectly unless it be known of what it is a sign.*[15] Man refers beyond the significative unity of that which is understood by the reflexive acts of intellect to the efficient and final cause of this unity.[16] He infers, moreover, that this unity of diverse formal acts in the significative function of mind is a sign, and that that of which it is the sign is God.

Thus it is that thought willing to fix attention on itself, remembering itself and knowing itself therefrom, understands itself and enjoys or loves itself. But it thereby also comes to remember, understand, and love Him by whom mind was created and by whose continuous act of creation man's nature is sustained in being. In this interior sacramental and speculative act the mind makes itself wise and is made wise, wherewith it brings into efficient and formal action within itself the gift of grace which is through Christ, the Interior Master. ". . . from very God is not only nature, whereby He made us like His

the treatise *On the Immortality of the Soul.* This modification adds an extra dimension to the Platonic theory of reminiscence and the doctrine of innate ideas, since the veridical problem is adjusted to the metaphysics of being through God as the efficient and formal creator of natures.

[14] Cf. *On the Quantity of the Soul,* Ch. 29. *On the True Religion,* Ch. 32. *On Order,* Bk. II, Ch. 12. *On Free Will,* Bk. II, Ch. 8.

[15] *On the Trinity,* Bk. X, Ch. 1, § 2; Ch. 10, § 16.

[16] *On the Trinity,* Bk. XV.

image which is reason, by virtue of which we know Him, but from Him there is also grace, by virtue of which we are blessed through being united to Him." [17]

The movement towards unity through the reduction of diversity to order is intrinsic to man's nature in general, but in the significative dimension of his nature it has a possible freedom of movement over and above the economy of man's animal nature. True things are true precisely in the measure in which they *are* and are one, and simultaneously this is their measure of good or degree of completion.[18] In the motions of man's thought, which are free from the specious immediacy of the here and now, each level of cognition reflects within itself the transcendental properties of being, unity and truth.

If any similitude adequately resemble that of which it is the similitude, it is true relative to that which it resembles. Thus truth is a relation of adequacy between a sign or formal act and that which is signified by the sign or formal act of cognition.[19] A sign, it should be recalled, in its interior structure is a formal act of cognizing and involves a mode or modes of reference to that which is signified. Signs of corporeal things invade the senses and are appropriated through sensitive acts of attention; signs of intellective things or entities of reason are derived through thought reflecting on itself. Memory retains from both sensation and reflection, since in memory are stored in a latent state, apt for recall, the signs of past operations. The Augustinian levels of signification are outlined in this section: ". . . whether those things are present which are seen also by the bodily eye, or perceived by the other senses; or whether they are not present, but their likenesses are discerned by thought; or whether neither

---

[17] *City of God*, Bk. VIII, Ch. 10.

[18] *On the True Religion*, Ch. 36. *On the Trinity*, Bk. VIII, Ch. 1. *Enchiridion*, Chs. 12–14. *City of God*, Bk. IX, Ch. 16; Bk. XI, Ch. 27; Bk. XII, Chs. 2, 5.

[19] *On the Trinity*, Bk. VI, Ch. 10, § 11; Bk. IX, Chs. 11, 12.

of these is the case, but things are thought of which are neither bodily things or similitudes of bodily things, as the virtues and vices; or whether it be those things which are the subjects of instruction and of liberal disciplines; or whether the higher causes and reasons themselves of all things in the unchangeable nature are thought of . . ." On each level, knowing is a kind of referential vision concerned with modes of signifying.[20] The thread which runs through the quotation is that of the ways "in which things signify one thing by another." [21]

Signifying, then, begins with the invasion of sense by the sensible thing at one extreme of cognition in perceptive intuition and ends at the other extreme of cognition in intellectual intuition. It has been said earlier that similarity is a mean between complete alterity or diversity on the one hand and complete unity on the other. This applies to the contrary poles of the diversity of sense data and the unity of reflective assimilation. Between the extremes of intuitive perception and intellective unity intervene the liberal disciplines as utilities or instruments for ordering the intrication and extrication of sign-references.[22] But now it is time to investigate the order of signation more closely, and this will involve the liberal disciplines.

III

THE PROBLEM OF SIGNATION AND THE LIBERAL DISCIPLINES

The arts are formal instruments by which man explores the truth. When the language of temporally eventful truth is translated into the language of non-temporal truth, it may lead upon further speculation to the anagogic grasp of wisdom which is

[20] *On the Trinity*, Bk. XV, Chs. 9, 10, 11, 12.

[21] *On the Trinity*, Bk. XV, Ch. 9.

[22] St. Augustine designates the liberal disciplines as (1) grammar, rhetoric, and logic; (2) geometry, arithmetic, music, and astronomy. Cf. *On Order*, Bk. I, Ch. 9; Bk. II, Chs. 12, 13, 14, 15. *De musica*, Book VI.

from God. Hence, the arts are formal disciplines by means of which man develops skills from aptitudes and at the same time is made wise and makes himself wise. The treatise *On Free Will* establishes the condition that truth reveals the good. The *De ordine,* the *De magistro,* and the *De musica* teach that the liberal disciplines are skill utilities or formal instruments for the mastery of truth. The treatise *On the Immortality of the Soul* indicates how the formal arts are employed in the anagogic functions of theology.

In order to secure a certain detachment from the immediacy of our discussion, we shall consider a brief synopsis of the scope of the arts. The *natural arts* are concerned with the orderly repetitive changes of nature. These are veiled or vestigial signs. The task of the liberal arts is to translate them into simple signs and formulæ of such signs, namely, into steady and luminous symbols of thought. The *useful arts* consist of the regimented manipulative acts of man, established by training, through which tools are employed as a means to certain productive ends. The grasp and formulation of these regimented acts depend on the liberal arts. By means of the liberal arts things manipulated by the exterior man are formulated by the interior man, with the help of analytic reflection ordered to truth as regulated by the formal modes of language and mathematics. The *fine arts,* aside from æsthetic considerations, consist of those skilled and orderly operations which treat particular things in such sort that the particular things refer to themselves significatively and also refer beyond themselves to other things. Here again formulation above the level of making requires the liberal arts, which sharpen the insights and distinctions involved in the particular thing. The *practical arts* (prudence: social and personal action) consist in the true and reasoned state of a capacity to act with regard to human goods, involving opinions or the problematical. Prudence governs the social sciences. The *scientific arts* consist in the state of the capacity to demonstrate by induction and syllogism, involving knowledge of the true and necessary. The *philosophical* or *speculative arts* consist in the intuitive grasp of first principles and the scientific knowledge of things highest by nature. The *theological arts* consist in the state of the capacity to render revelation intelligible in revealed theology and to render revealed theology evidential by analogies taken from the other arts as through natural theology.

The order or compendence of the arts is the order of man's virtues, capacities, or aptitudes, and through the development of the arts virtues are actualized and *vice versa*. To use a Kantian expression, the deduction of the ordered possibilities of the arts is a deduction of man's intrinsic perfectibility, for the arts are modes of human action by which human beings approach the perfection of man as man.

The rational means or formal instruments presupposed for the above order of arts are the liberal arts or disciplines. There are seven of these and they fall into two groups. The first group is the trivium which consists of *grammar,* the art and science of concrete things, elements or principles, as they are assimilated through acts of cognition and employed in mediums of discourse; *rhetoric,* the art and science of applying the terms of grammar, both concrete and abstract, for practical and theoretical ends; *logic,* the art and science of discovering and applying abstract forms. The second group is the quadrivium which consists of *arithmetic* or theory of ratios, *geometry* or ratios applied to figures, *music* or ratios applied to changing things, *astronomy* or ratios applied to geometrical things in motion. The liberal disciplines contain the basic languages by means of which all arts are intelligible and formulable in mediums of discourse. Their perfection is intimate to man's perfection, since as rational arts they stand as instruments to man's interior virtues or powers. The development and exercise of the liberal arts or disciplines facilitate the mastery of the other arts, and, since the arts are developed and perfected each by each and each by all, the scope and function of man's aptitudes are developed and completed in the same ratios. Man's nature is perfected by the mastery and exercise of formal disciplines which exist in and through the ordered formal acts of the interior man. This develops the implications of St. Augustine's statement that the individual man lives well when he lives according to the image of the interior man, which image is the image of God.

Since the function of grammar is a matter of special attention in the *De magistro*, we shall discuss here only grammar, rhetoric, and logic. The *De magistro*, however modest it may be in its scope and function, is basic for the mastery of Augustinian doctrine. Let us, then, restate briefly the salient features of the trivium. Signation means the operation of certain things which are able to signify certain other things. The operations of particular things (the elements, principles, or incomplex terms of discourse) fall within the domain of grammar. The signifying of certain particular things by certain other particular things in mediums of discourse is called rhetoric. The relationships of particular things to common orders is called logic.

The psychological deduction enters here as an account of the order of coming to know. In Book X of his treatise *On the Trinity*, St. Augustine gives a synoptic picture of the routine of coming to be known which is ordered thus: a thing in physical nature is to a bodily sense as a similitude of a natural thing in memory is to the eye of the mind (*acies*). By an act of the will distinctive attention is brought to bear upon the sensible thing as sensed, and a sensation is generated. The sense is the corporeal *instrument by virtue of which,* and the sense as a corporeal instrument is transformed by the sensible thing; but sensation is actually initiated through the will, which operates efficiently as an animate principle upon the physically trans-

formed sense. Thus, as St. Augustine asserts, the sense is corporeal but it is also animated; hence, sense is a middle term
between the sensible thing and the animate efficiency of the
soul. As a corporeal thing the sense organ is in relation to a
sensible thing; as simultaneously subject to the efficient action
of the soul, however, it is animated. The sense organ is *both*
corporeal *and* animated, so that, consequently, the sense organ
rendered animate by the soul acts as such in regard to the soul.
It is, then, the will which fixes attention upon the sense in-
formed, so that the transformed similitude of the sensible thing
is retained in memory. St. Augustine observes that the moment
of sensation is so immediate that only by an act of analysis is it
possible to distinguish the sensible thing from the transformed
sense and from the similitude of the transformed sense which is
retainable.

The image or similitude in memory is assimilated to the
vision of the mind (*acies*) by a further act of efficient attention.
Again the terms of this distinction seem so exceedingly alike
that analytic attention must form a distinction. By distinctive
moments we move from the image in the eye to the image
retained in memory, and then to the formal similitude in the
vision of the mind. But we note that the acts of attention imply
that reflective acts of analysis are involved, which suggests that
the mind is formally and constructively active in this process.
Mind is a single substance, so that, therefore, we must distinguish analytically its double function as vested in the order of
coming to know and in the formal order or act itself of knowing. For St. Augustine it is necessary to introduce the dimensions of formal signs between the order of coming to know and
the order of knowing. We may recall Plato's injunction that
between shadows and ideas intervene the 'mathematicals' as a
basic language by means of which the temporal and contingent
is translated into the necessary and eternal.

Let us briefly restate the above discussion, not in regard to the psychogenetic order of coming to have knowledge, but in regard to the formal causes of knowing. The particulars of discourse, signs, invade the sense organs, and the animate principle as both efficient and formal meets this invasion by means of the distinctions of signifying, that is, by the liberal disciplines. From the point of view of the natural world which is a network of analogies, the above statement implies that terms of analogies enter the senses, and as a result elements are transmitted to analytic attention for discrimination and reintegration. The trivium, for example, elaborates this material by an orderly analysis of it. When a sensation or image (similitude) is perceived as an instance of knowledge, or as having some ratio to a natural object, it is said to be imposed as a sign on its object. This vertical relation is implicitly analogical or *ratio*nal in character, and it is rendered definite or determinate by the sort of analysis featured here. When a sign through a formal or analytic act of cognition is imposed on its thing, it is said to have *first imposition*. Thus a first imposition refers beyond itself to the natural thing which it signifies. After this when the image as a first impositional sign is retained in memory, a second act of distinction may follow whereby the image or formal act of cognition may be understood as referring to itself. When the sign or formal act of cognition is known through itself and by itself reflexively, it is said to have *second imposition*. For St. Augustine this is executed through the interior sense which knows both the acts of the senses and its own acts.

But the question of conventional notations complicates matters here, because of the fact that written words, spoken words, and gestures are sorts of signs. Let us once more list the kinds of signs: (1) *Natural signs,* belonging to the analogical network of nature, are preformed things or sensibles which invade the senses. They are not made by man, but rather they are said to

be discovered. (2) *Cognitive signs* are formal acts of signification by which distinctions are made in that which is retained in
sensation. These explicate the formal import of acts of sensation.
(3) *Conventional signs* are factives or notations associated with
cognitive signs, such as written letter combinations, spoken
syllables, gestures, etc. These have real reference through and
only through the cognitive signs and their modes of signifying
that which is signified (the signifiable). A science of grammar
may be constructed in terms of *con*notations; e. g., *lion* is a *noun*,
and *fierce* is an *adjective*. Thus the science of grammar in this
sense deals with the operations whereby the relations of words
and sentences are determined. Its method is that of comparison
by means of which the relations underlying communication are
formulated. This suggests an analogy between the analogies of
words and the analogies intrinsic to cognitive signs. But grammar as a science, nevertheless, is not itself a science of natural
things, but rather a formulation through and by virtue of the
modes of cognition of a parallel notation for sorts of references.
For a notation to be significant in regard to natural things,
either to the agent who uses it or to the recipient who assimilates
it, involves a formal act of cognition; but a formal act of cognition may signify and be intelligible without the interposition
of a conventional sign. The reader will be able to explore the
more intricate details of this as stated in terms of teaching in the
De magistro.

In speaking of first and second impositions, we have so far
concerned ourselves with signifying functions which fall within
the scope of the exterior man of sensation and sensible memory.
With certain restrictions, animals may be said to share the
functions of sensation and sensible memory with man. Reason,
however, is man's specifying attribute, and it involves a dimension of signifying over and above the functions of the exterior
man. It is formally provoked by the signs or images in sensible

memory; by an efficient act of the will the analytic functions of reason are fixed upon the occasional data. The barbarians of sense invade a land of sophisticated culture with the result that they are assimilated through its arts and laws inasmuch as these arts and laws bear a certain conformity to the natures which are assimilated.

By virtue of the spontaneity of reason, we intuit, classify, calculate, demonstrate, and know in a formal sense beyond the level of impositions, that is, in terms of the distinction between *first* and *second intentions*. Between the terms of the analogies which lie behind and include our first and second impositional acts there are latent ratios of signification. These call for explication as universals. Analytic attention meets this demand in two ways: (1) by ordering particulars in classes and series; (2) by reflexively knowing these in and through themselves. Thus in terms of St. Augustine's account of sensible memory the images of sensible things are compared and contrasted in terms of *same* and *other,* their similarities and differences are noted, and they are ordered accordingly. We may distinguish, for example, the genus and species of a floral or faunal thing, come to know it as such, and recognize in its first intentional structure, by analogy to other first intentional structures, a common similitude of universal form. Second intentions land us in formal logic proper. Through these formal cognitive acts of analysis and reference, reason secures the incomplex terms, elements or principles of general discourse which enter into propositional complexes. The propositional logic of predication or attribution is able to explicate on this basis in terms of predetermined analogical matrices without a confusion of sign references or types. From the expansion of intentional analogies (which are ratios or modes of signification intrinsic to the simple elements of cognition) is derived the foundation of functional and propositional formulations.

Our analysis above the level of first and second impositions has exceeded what St. Augustine actually formulates in the *De magistro,* but it does not exceed what he implicitly suggests. The advantage of stating the distinctive functions of the first and second intentions consists in the fact that the impositional operations are brought into clearer relief as subordinate acts of discrimination in the order of knowing significatively.

We may now consider rhetoric as the methodical rotation and translation of the signifying terms involved in impositions, and these analytic motions are undertaken for the purpose of elaborating the intentional significance of the signs as factors in a significant whole. Rhetoric turns a sign or center of signification through all the possible phases of signifying, thus passing from one signifying aspect to another, noting and completing the ratios of similarity and difference involved in the simple terms. Logic has two uses: (1) to formulate the modes of signification into universal orders; (2) to guide concrete thinking so that it moves in conformity with ordered ideas, as in dialectic. The general features of our discussion may be summarized by means of a convenient quotation. "The liberal arts are practised well by those who have the intellectual virtues, but the liberal arts and sciences are also the disciplines by which one achieves the intellectual virtues. Art is an intellectual virtue, that is, a capacity connected with the senses, imagination, and sentiments to do grammar, that is, to arrange and make changing things that will carry significance. Practical wisdom is the trained capacity to operate with opinion, the medium in which rhetoric moves; it is the capacity to make and to respond to rhetoric. The impositions of rhetoric and grammar bog down and collapse unless they are kept straight and are obedient to the intentions as they are exercised in intellectual intuition and in science. Philosophical wisdom may depend on illumination, but it does not operate except through the liberal arts. Dialectic is the practice of philosophical wisdom in so far as philosophical wisdom becomes explicit knowledge." [23] This excludes the modern version of the two truths, the split-personality of the modern expert (or even *Gelehrter*) between the sort of virtue which he does possess and the sorts of virtue which remain dormant in his undeveloped aptitudes.

It is sufficiently evident that for St. Augustine the arts and sciences are the formal instruments of truth and hence of knowledge. Truth illumines the way to beatitude and in so doing develops the intrinsic aptitudes of man as man. St. Augustine points out that a doctrine, which is a complex network of signs and things signated (whether things, ideas or other sorts of signs), is an indivisible totality as it is in itself.[24] Now an angel because of its nature could know a doctrine as an indivisible unity in a single moment of intuition. But the rational animal man is something inferior to an angel and something superior to a brute. As something less than an angel, he cannot grasp truth in its instantaneous extensity and intensity, but, as something more than a brute, he can achieve a certain discursive unity in diversity as a result of coöperating formal acts of cognition.[25] Man must know through the canons of the liberal arts, since the liberal arts deal with the diverse formal modes by which man constructs or discovers doctrines.

Now if, as St. Augustine asserts, the supreme good is one to all, and one and true are convertible, each with each, and each with a mode of being, then the truth in which the good exists must be one and the same to all.[26] Thought produces from a

---

[23] From an unpublished typescript by Scott M. Buchanan.

[24] *De musica*, Bk. VI, Ch. 16, § 55. *On the Trinity*, Bks. XI and XII; Bk. XV, Chs. 14–16. *On the Quantity of the Soul*, Ch. 25.

[25] *On Order*, Bk. II, Chs. 16–19. *On Free Will*, Bk. II.

[26] *On the True Religion*, Chs. 23, 32, 36. *On Order*, Bk. II, Chs. 16–19. *On Free Will*, Bk. II, Ch. 12. *On the Trinity*, Bk. VI, Chs. 4, 14–16. *On the Morals of the Church*, Bk. I, Ch. 15.

formal analysis of its operations canons for controlling its materials of knowledge. Herein lies man's freedom, since a thing is free when it operates according to rules derived from its own nature. Modes of knowing when reduced to such rules have an analogical conformity in the formal acts of man as man and hence in the acts of all men. For this reason, however great the diversity of what is knowable may be, self-disciplined minds possess a common stock of formal instruments through which diversity may be reduced to intelligible unity. Man need not be at the mercy of diversity, nor yet undervalue the significance of diversity, if he possesses formal skills by which diversity may be rendered commonly formulable, luminous, and symbolically explicated through generic modes of understanding. St. Augustine's expression "liberal disciplines" is seen to be analogous to and implicated with his expression *liberum arbitrium,* the free or liberal will.

For St. Augustine the language skills are not only concerned with the exigencies of basic daily routine, but in addition they are acutely involved with the formal and efficient nature of the mind and hence with its health. To neglect this aspect of St. Augustine's wisdom is to miss the interior principle which animates and sustains his whole doctrine and so to miss the intrinsic links which bind his speculations into the chain of the scholastic tradition. Not only is God one being to all, but the formal means which lead to knowing what is knowable of Him to finite man are one, same and common to all men.

In the Augustinian picture the world is a network of traces, obscure similarities of God, signs created by Him and hence signs reflecting His nature, to be appropriated by man and rendered intelligible by the arts. And, moreover, Scripture is filled with words, the messages of which need to be unlocked by the liberal arts as food for contemplation and moral instruction. Other books are located in an analogous problematical medium. Between the knowable of discourse and the mind which knows by interior acts intervene the liberal disciplines which rule and inform the interior acts through the very functional structure of the acts themselves.

The task of translation and interpretation is as omnipresent as God's creative act and man's appropriation, but man, who lacks the angelic excellence for knowing, must know by diverse modes of signifying and must understand through the discipline of these modes. Step by step, mode by mode, to reduce his confusion of the divine data to unity and order is the pain of man's imperfection but also the dignity of his nature. Of animate material things only man is made to know his destiny and to love God intelligently. The autonomy of intelligence is coöperative with the actions of will, and the one and the other mutually sustain and strengthen each other. St. Augustine discovered the significance of the liberal disciplines where the Greeks had discovered it, that is, in the very center of the metaphysics of conversion or being. But he did something which extends beyond the Greeks by adjusting the metaphysics of conversion to the theology of grace. This master of a Platonizing tendency exceeded the wisdom of his traditional masters and ordered the arts to a new sort of urgency.

It is of the very essence of human nature that in man the liberal disciplines, with their formal means for perfecting aptitudes or virtues, are instruments to man's perfection as man. Certainly, it follows as a corollary that when the arts and sciences are dispersed, confused, or distorted, as for instance from neglect, or if not from neglect then from the overemphasis of specialists, they are corrupt. When this is the case man's instruments to self-realization are in the same unhealthy state. Rousseau, for one, understood the general import of man's corruption through that very civilization which should advance him. St. Augustine taught that man's corrupted free will needs the Physician of Grace. And he caught the analogy of corrupted free will to arts which are not perfected. The Physician of Grace as interpreted under one analogy renders the will relatively perfectible, whereas the Interior Master as interpreted under another analogy renders the Law relatively perfectible through the utility of the arts. Christ is both the Physician of Grace and the Interior Master who works through man's intrinsic nature. The analogy of grace and the analogy of law are seen to have a common being in Christ, who is the intermediary by whom man is redeemed from his errors and indecisions. The doctrine of St. Augustine is inclusive for thought and for action.

* * *

The following translations of the *De magistro* and the *De immortalitate animae* have been undertaken with the view of presenting the liberal arts student with simple texts of two of St. Augustine's works not at present conveniently available. In a greater or less degree the two works are both expository for the liberal arts and exemplary models of them, properties which have dictated their selection as texts for students of the liberal arts. According to report St. Augustine wrote a treatise on each of the seven liberal arts, but of these none is positively known to have survived with the exception of the *De musica*.

It has been necessary to sacrifice literary grace to other considerations in the medium of translation, and the reason for this is doubtless evident enough. "For it is in the highest degree useful to . . . men to come to know how ideas are to be preferred to words, just as the soul is preferred to the body. And from this, too, it follows that they ought to wish to listen to discourses remarkable for their truth, rather than to those which are notable for their eloquence; just as they ought to be anxious to have friends illustrious for their wisdom, rather than those whose capital merit is their beauty." Thus St. Augustine teaches in his manual *On the Catechizing of the Uninstructed* (Ch. 9).

The writer of this preface gratefully acknowledges the help he has derived from his predecessors, many of whom are cited in the bibliography. He is, moreover, greatly indebted to his wife, who has assisted him with the entire task of preparing the texts. The writer is indebted in general to the intellectual virtue and creative imagination of Scott M. Buchanan, and it is an especial pleasure to acknowledge this debt.

The texts employed in translation are those contained in the corpus *Opera et Studio Monachorum Ordinis Sancti Benedicti (e Congregatione S. Mauri), Editio Parisina altera, emendata et aucta. Tomus Primus, Parisis, apud Gaume Fratres, Bibliopolas,* M DCCC XXXVI. *S. Aur. Augustini, Hipponensis Episcopi, OPERA OMNIA.* Notes in the text proper are confined to those given in the originals. At the end of the text will be found a chronological chart of the main events circumstantial to the life of St. Augustine as well as a citation of the order and probable time of his major works. The introductory essay, like prefaces in general, requires some apology. Economy of space has dictated a radical foreshortening of exposition, which tends to cramp the intervals of discussion. But, conceivably, it stresses certain aspects of Augustinian thought which, although to the writer they seem to have been long uncultivated, are of primary importance. If, then, the Preface provokes a certain suggestibility of implications, it will have rendered its suitable service.

GEORGE G. LECKIE

Brooklin,
Maine.

CONCERNING THE TEACHER

(*De magistro*)
ONE BOOK
(Written about 389 A. D.)

CONCERNING THE TEACHER

(A Dialogue)

Persons Represented: ⎰ AUGUSTINE
⎱ ADEODATUS, aged fifteen years, son of Augustine.

CHAPTER I

THE PURPOSE OF SPEECH

1. Aug.—What does it seem to you that we wish to accomplish when we speak?

Ad.—As it occurs to me now, either to teach or to learn.

Aug.—I see, and I agree to one of these points. For it is evident that when we speak we wish to teach. But how do we learn?

Ad.—How, indeed, except by asking questions?

Aug.—Even then, as I understand it, we only wish to teach. For, I ask, do you question for any other reason except that you may teach what you wish to him you question? *Certainly*

Ad.—That is true.

Aug.—So now, you do see that in speaking we desire only that we may teach.

Ad.—That is not clear to me: for, if speaking is only expressing words, it is evident that we do that when we sing. And since we often sing when we are alone, with no one present to learn, it does not seem to me that we wish to teach anything.

Aug.—Ah, but I think there is a certain kind of teaching by

3

means of reminding, indeed a very important kind, which will be revealed in this dialogue of ours. But if you do not think that we learn when we remember things, and that the man does not teach who reminds, I shall not object. And now I posit two reasons for speaking: either that we may teach, or that we may remind either others or ourselves; and the latter is what we do when we sing. Or does it not seem so to you?

Ad.—Not exactly. For it is quite seldom that I sing to remind myself; it is usually only to give myself pleasure.

Aug.—I see what you mean. But do you not see that what pleases you in singing is a certain modulation of sound. And, since this can be either added to or separated from the words, is not speaking one thing and singing another? For there are songs on pipes and on the cithara, and birds sing, and occasionally we, too, make musical sounds without words. This sound can be called singing, but it cannot be called speaking. Or have you any objection against this?

Ad.—None that matters.

2. *Aug.*—You do agree, then, that speaking is undertaken only for the sake of reminding or of teaching?

Ad.—It would seem so were I not troubled that while we are praying we are certainly speaking, and yet it is not right to believe that God is either taught anything by us or that He is reminded.

Aug.—It seems you do not know that we have been taught to pray in our secret closets,[1] by which is meant the inmost part of the mind, for the sole reason that God does not need to be reminded or taught by our speech in order that He may fulfil our desires. For he who speaks expresses the sign of his will by means of articulate sound. But God should be sought and entreated in the very secret places of the rational soul, which is called

---

[1] Matthew, VI, 6.

the interior man; for He wished this to be His temple. Have you not read in the Apostle: "Know ye not that ye are the temple of God, and that the spirit of God dwelleth in you?" [2] And also: "Christ dwells in the inner man." [3] And have you not observed, in the Psalm: "Commune with your own heart upon your bed, and be still. Offer the sacrifices of righteousness, and put your trust in the Lord." [4] Where, then, is a sacrifice of righteousness made, unless in the temple of the mind and in the chambers of the heart? And the place for sacrifice is also the place for prayer. Consequently, there is no need to speak when we pray, that is, with spoken words, unless perhaps for the sake of indicating, as the priests do, what is in our minds, not in order that God may hear, but that men may hear, and, through being reminded, may by their consent be lifted up to God. Or do you object?

Ad.—I entirely agree.

Aug.—Does it not trouble you that the Great Master, when He taught the disciples to pray, taught them certain words? [5] Such instruction seems only to have taught how we ought to speak in prayer.

Ad.—That does not disturb me at all. For He did not teach them words, but taught them things by means of the words in order that they might remind themselves to whom and for what purpose they ought to pray when they do so in those inner sanctuaries of the mind.

Aug.—You understand that correctly. For I believe that you observe, at the same time, that even when one formulates a statement, although we utter no sound, yet because we think words we speak within the mind. And so in all speech we only remind, since memory, within which words inhere, by revolving them

[2] I Corinthians, III, 16.
[3] Ephesians, III, 17.
[4] Psalm IV, 5, 6.
[5] Matthew, VI, 9.

causes to come into the mind the very things of which the words are signs.

Ad.—I understand and follow you.

CHAPTER II

MAN SHOWS THE MEANING OF WORDS ONLY THROUGH WORDS

3. Aug.—Then we agree that words are signs?

Ad.—We do agree.

Aug.—But what about this? Can a sign be a sign unless it signifies something?

Ad.—It cannot.

Aug.—How many words are in this line: *Si nihil ex tanta superis placet urbe relinqui?* [6]

Ad.—Eight.

Aug.—Then there are eight signs?

Ad.—That is so.

Aug.—I believe you understand this line.

Ad.—Quite well, I think.

Aug.—Then tell me what each word signifies.

Ad.—Indeed, I see what *si* [if] signifies, but I cannot find another word by which to explain it.

Aug.—Whatever may be signified by the word, at least you know where it is.

Ad.—It seems to me that *si* [if] signifies doubt, and where is doubt except in the mind?

Aug.—I accept that for the time being. Go on with the others.

Ad.—What does *nihil* [nothing] signify except that which is not?

[6] *Æneid*, Bk. II, line 659.

Aug.—Perhaps you are right. But I cannot agree with you because of your recent admission, namely, that a sign is not a sign unless it signifies something. And that which is not cannot in any way be something. Accordingly, the second word in the line is not a sign because of the fact that it does not signify anything, which would mean that we have agreed falsely that all words are signs or that every sign signifies something.

Ad.—Indeed, you press too hard. But when we do not express what we signify, any word which we utter is simply nonsense. Yet I believe that as you are now speaking to me, you do not utter nonsense, but that by each word from your lips you give a sign to me in order that I may understand something. Consequently, you ought not to express the two syllables *nihil* [nothing] when you speak if you do not signify anything by means of them. But if you see that a necessary expression is made by means of them, and that we are taught or reminded of something when they strike the ear, then you likewise see just what I wish to say but cannot explain.

Aug.—What shall we do? Since the mind does not see the thing and yet finds, or thinks that it finds, that it does not exist, can we not say that a certain affection of the mind is signified rather than a thing which is not?

Ad.—Perhaps that is just what I was trying to explain.

Aug.—Let us proceed then, be that matter as it may, lest a very silly thing happen to us.

Ad.—What, pray?

Aug.—Lest nothing should detain us, and we should suffer delay.

Ad.—That is indeed ridiculous; and yet I see that it can happen, although I do not know how. Ah, but indeed, I see clearly that it has happened.

4. *Aug.*—In due order, God willing, this sort of confusion

will be clearer. Now go back to the line and try, as well as you can, to explain what the other words in it signify.

Ad.—The third is a preposition *ex* [from] for which we can, I think, say *de* [from].

Aug.—I am not asking you to replace one well known word with another equally well known word which means the same thing; granted indeed that it does mean the same thing, which for the present we shall allow. Surely, if the poet had not expressed it *ex tanta urbe,* but *de tanta,* and if I were to ask you what *de* means, you might say *ex,* and we should then have two words, or signs, signifying, as you think, the same one thing. But I am asking about that one thing itself, whatever it is, which is signified by these two words.

Ad.—It appears to mean a sort of separation from a thing in which something has been, though the thing no longer remains, as in this line, for example: although the city was destroyed, perhaps a few Trojans were left from the city [*ex illa*]; or, if the thing does remain, as when we say, for example, that there are traders in Africa from the city of Rome [*ex urbe Roma*].

Aug.—I admit that, and I prefer not to enumerate how many exceptions may be found to your rule. But, surely, you readily observe that you have expounded words with words, signs with signs, things well known by means of things likewise well known. I wish, however, that you would show me, if you can, the things themselves of which these are the signs.

CHAPTER III

WHETHER ANYTHING CAN BE SHOWN WITHOUT A SIGN

5. *Ad.*—I wonder that you do not know, or that you pretend not to know, that what you wish cannot be done by my answers

as long as we are engaged in discussion, since while we are actually discussing I cannot answer except in words. You seek the things, however, which, whatever they are, are surely not words, and yet you also ask me about them by means of words. Do first ask me about them without the help of words, and I shall then reply in the same way.

Aug.—I admit that you are within your right. But if when *paries* [wall] is expressed, I should ask you what the three syllables mean, could you not point it out with your finger so that I might see the very thing itself of which the three-syllable word is a sign? You would show it to me, and yet you would not employ words.

Ad.—I admit that it can be done, but only in the case of nouns [names] by means of which bodies are signified, provided the bodies themselves are present.

Aug.—Do we not call color a certain quality of a body, rather than a body?

Ad.—That is so.

Aug.—Then why cannot this be shown by pointing the finger? Or do you also add to bodies the qualities of bodies, since, for example, when colors are present they can be shown quite as well without words?

Ad.—When I said bodies I meant all corporeal things, that is, all things which are sensed in bodies.

Aug.—But consider now: should you not make some exceptions?

Ad.—You advise me well. For I should not say all corporeal things, but all visible things. For I confess that sound, odor, taste, weight, and others of this sort which pertain to other senses, although they cannot be sensed without bodies, still they cannot be shown by pointing the finger.

Aug.—Have you not seen men when they discourse, so to speak, by means of gestures with those who are deaf, the deaf likewise using gestures? Do they not question and reply and teach and indicate everything they wish or at least a great many things? When they use gestures they do not merely indicate visible things, but also sounds and tastes and other things of this sort. For actors in the theater present and exhibit entire dramas for the most part by means of pantomime without using words.

Ad.—I have no objection to make except that neither I nor even a pantomimic actor himself can show you without words what *ex* [from] signifies.

6. *Aug.*—Perhaps that is true. But let us fancy that he can. You do not doubt, I think, that whatever bodily movement the pantomimic actor may use in order to show me the thing signified by the word, the motion will not be the thing itself but a sign. Consequently the motion, though not indicating a word by means of a word, will nevertheless indicate a sign by a sign. The monosyllable *ex* and the gesture will both mean one and the same thing, which is what I wish to have shown me in some other way than by making a sign.

Ad.—How, I pray, can what you ask be done?

Aug.—In the same way in which the wall was shown.

Ad.—Not even a wall can be shown without a sign, as far as I can see from our discussion at this point. For the directing of the finger is certainly not the wall, but through it a sign is given by which the wall may be seen. I see nothing, therefore, which can be shown without signs.

Aug.—What if I were to ask you what walking is, and you should get up and walk. Would it not be shown me through the thing itself rather than through words, or would you use some other signs?

Ad.—I admit that point, and I am ashamed not to have seen so obvious a thing. From this thousands of other things now occur to me which can be shown through themselves [*per se*] and not through signs, as eating, drinking, sitting, standing, shouting and innumerable others.

Aug.—Come now, tell me; if I, knowing absolutely nothing of the meaning of the word, should ask you while you are in the act of walking what walking is, how would you teach me?

Ad.—I should walk somewhat more quickly in order that after your question your attention might be directed to something new. And yet I should do only what was to be shown.

Aug.—Do you know that walking is one thing and hurrying another? For he who walks need not immediately hurry, and he who hurries does not necessarily walk, since we speak of hurrying in writing and reading and in innumerable other things. Hence, if after my question you were to do more quickly what you were doing already, I should think walking to be merely hurrying. Hurrying would be the new thing added, and so I should be misled by that.

Ad.—I admit that we cannot show a thing without a sign if we are questioned while we are in the act of doing it. For if we add nothing, the questioner will think that we do not wish to show him and will suppose that, to ridicule him, we are continuing what we are doing. But if he asks about things which we are able to do, and yet does not ask while we are in the act of doing them, we can, by doing what he asks after his question, show him what he asks by means of the thing itself rather than by a sign. Unless perhaps the questioner should ask me what speaking is while I am in the act of speaking; since when I say anything in order to teach him the answer to this question it is necessary for me to speak. If this happens, I shall teach him until I make clear to him what he wants to know, adhering to the thing itself which he desires to have shown him and not casting about beyond the thing itself for some sign by which I may indicate it.

CHAPTER IV

WHETHER SIGNS ARE SHOWN BY SIGNS

7. *Aug.*—Very keen, indeed. Now, then, are we in agreement that those things can be shown without signs, which either we are not doing when we are asked but can do at once, or which themselves are signs (as in speaking). For when we speak we make signs, and this is called signifying.

Ad.—It is agreed.

Aug.—If certain signs are asked about, then these signs can be shown by means of signs. But when things which are not signs are asked about, they can be shown either by means of doing them after the question, if they can be done, or by giving signs by means of which they can be called to the attention.

Ad.—That is so.

Aug.—In this threefold division let us first consider this, namely, that signs are shown by means of signs. For words are not the only signs, are they?

Ad.—No.

Aug.—Now it seems to me that in speaking we signify by means of words either words themselves or other signs, as, for instance, when we say "gesture" or "letter" (for the things which are signified by the words *gesture* or *letter* are also signs); or we signify something else which is not a sign, as when we say "stone," for this word is a sign since it signifies something, but that which is signified in this case is not in turn a sign. But this genus, that is, the genus in which things which are not signs are signified by words, does not belong to the present part of our discussion. For we have undertaken to consider that genus in which signs are shown by means of signs, and in it we have discovered two parts, since through signs we teach or call to mind either the same signs or other signs. Or does it not seem so to you?

Ad.—It is obvious.

8. *Aug.*—Then tell me to what sense pertain the signs which are words.

Ad.—To hearing.

Aug.—And gesture?

Ad.—To sight.

Aug.—What do we find about written words? Are they not better understood as signs of words than as words? A word is that which is uttered by the articulate voice with some meaning, but the voice can be perceived only by the sense of hearing. It thus happens that when a word is read a sign is made in the eyes by which that sign which pertains to the ears comes into the mind.

Ad.—I agree entirely.

Aug.—I think you agree also when I say that the word *name* [noun] signifies something to us.

Ad.—Truly it does.

Aug.—What then?

Ad.—To be sure, that which something is called, as *Romulus, Rome, virtue, river,* and innumerable others.

Aug.—Do not these words signify things?

Ad.—Indeed they do signify things.

Aug.—Is there no difference between the names and the things which are signified by means of them?

Ad.—A great deal of difference.

Aug.—I should like to hear from you what it is.

Ad.—This, in the first place, that the former are signs, while the latter are not.

Aug.—Can we agree to call *signifiable* those things which can be signified by means of signs and yet are not signs, just as we call those things visible which can be seen, so that we may discuss these things more conveniently in proper order?

Ad.—It is quite agreeable.

Aug.—Are the four signs which you mentioned just above signified by no other signs?

Ad.—I am surprised you think I have forgotten that we found that written things are to things uttered by the voice as signs of signs.

Aug.—Tell me why they differ.

Ad.—Because the former are visible, the latter audible. For why should we not say audible if we say signifiable?

Aug.—I agree and thank you. But again, I ask, can these four signs be signified by no other audible signs, as you remember the visible signs can be?

Ad.—I also recall that this was said recently. For I answered that a noun [name] signifies something, and I had put the above four under its signification; both that [noun] and these things, if of course they be uttered by the voice, I understand to be audible.

Aug.—Now what is the difference between an audible sign and audible things signified which in turn are signs?

Ad.—Between what we call noun [name] and the four above which we put under its signification, I see this difference, that noun is an audible sign of audible signs, whereas those placed under its signification are audible signs of things: partly of visible things, as *Romulus* is, and *Rome,* and *river;* partly of intelligible things as *virtue* is.

9. *Aug.*—I accept and approve that. But do you know that all things which are uttered by the articulate voice with some signification are called words?

Ad.—I do.

Aug.—And so a noun [name] is a word, since we see that it is uttered with some signification by the articulate voice. And when we say that an eloquent man uses fair words, he also uses fair names, and when the slave in Terence's play said to the old lord, "I seek fair words," he had also expressed many nouns.[7]

Ad.—I agree.

Aug.—You grant, therefore, that by these two syllables which we pronounce when we say "verbum" [word] *name* [noun] is also signified, and that, accordingly, *word* is a sign of *name*.

Ad.—I agree.

Aug.—I also want you to answer this. Since *word* is a sign of *name,* and *name* is a sign of *river,* and *river* is a sign of a thing which can now be seen, so that between what can be seen and *river* which is its sign, and between this sign and the name which you have said to be its sign, there is a difference, what do you think is the difference between the sign of *name,* which we find to be *word,* and name itself of which it is the sign?

Ad.—I understand this difference, namely, that those things which are signified by *name* [noun] are also signified by *word,* for as *name* is a word, so also *river* is a word. Yet everything which is signified by means of a word is not signified by means of a noun. For *si* [if] which is at the inception of the line you mentioned, and *ex* [from], from the discussion of which we have been led by reason into these matters, are both words but not nouns; and many such are found. Consequently, since all nouns are words but not all words are nouns, it seems to me evident what I think the difference is between word and noun, that is, between the sign of that sign which signifies no other signs, and the sign of that sign which in turn signifies other signs.

Aug.—Do you grant that every horse is an animal, but that not every animal is a horse?

Ad.—Who doubts that?

Aug.—Then the difference between *noun* and *word* is the

[7] In *Andria,* act 1, scene 2, v. 33.

same as the difference between *horse* and *animal*. Perhaps, how-ever, you are prevented from agreeing because we speak of *verbum* [verb] in another way in which it signifies words which are declined by tenses, and these words are obviously not nouns.

Ad.—That is precisely the point which made me doubtful.

Aug.—Do not let that trouble you. For speaking in a gen-eral sense, we call signs all those things which signify some-thing, and words are included under this. Then, too, we say "military signs" or "banners," which are properly called signs, but words do not belong to this genus. And yet if I were to say that just as every horse is an animal but not every animal is a horse, so likewise every word is a sign but not every sign is a word, you would, I think, not doubt it.

Ad.—Now I understand and agree heartily that there is be-tween *verbum* [word] used generally and *noun* the same dif-ference which is between *animal* and *horse*.

10. Aug.—Do you also know that when we say "animal" this three-syllable word which is uttered by the voice is one thing and what it signifies is another?

Ad.—I have already agreed to that concerning all signs and things signifiable.

Aug.—Do all signs seem to you to signify something other than what they are, as when we say "animal" this three-syllable word in no way signifies what it is itself?

Ad.—Surely not, for when we say "sign" it signifies not only other signs, whatever they are, but it also signifies itself, for it is a word and all words certainly are signs.

Aug.—How then? When we say the two-syllable "verbum" [word], does not something of this sort happen? For if this two-syllable word signifies everything that is uttered by the articulate voice with some signification, it is also included in the genus.

Ad.—That is so.

Aug.—Is that not also true of *noun?* For it signifies nouns of all sorts, and *noun* [*nomen*] itself is a noun of the neuter gender. For if I should ask what part of speech a noun is, could you answer correctly anything except "noun"?

Ad.—That is true.

Aug.—Then there are signs which signify themselves along with the other things which they signify.

Ad.—There are.

Aug.—When we say "conjunctio" [conjunction], does it seem to you that this four-syllable word belongs to the above sort?

Ad.—Not at all, for those things which it signifies are not nouns, yet it is a noun.

CHAPTER V

RECIPROCAL SIGNS

11. Aug.—You have been properly attentive. Now see whether signs are found which signify each other mutually, so that however the former may be signified by the latter, the latter is likewise signified by the former. For the four-syllable word *conjunctio* [conjunction] and the things which are signified by it, as, for example, *si* [if], *vel* [or], *nam* [for], *namque* [for indeed], *nisi* [except], *ergo* [therefore], *quoniam* [whereas], and the like, are not reciprocal, since the items enumerated are signified by *conjunctio,* but it in turn is not signified by any of them.

Ad.—I see, and I desire to know what signs do signify each other mutually.

Aug.—You do know that when we say "noun" and "word" we say two words.

Ad.—I know that.

Aug.—Do you know that when we say "noun" and "word" we also say two nouns?

Ad.—I know that also.

Aug.—Then you know that *noun* is signified by means of a word, and *word* by means of a noun.

Ad.—I agree.

Aug.—Can you say, aside from the fact that they are written and pronounced differently, what is the difference between them?

Ad.—Perhaps I can. For I see that the difference is the same as that which I determined above. For when we express words, we signify everything which is uttered by the articulate voice with some signification; hence, every noun and *noun* itself is a word. But not every word is a noun, although *word* itself is a noun.

12. *Aug.*—If anyone should assert and maintain that every noun is a word and every word is a noun, would you be able to find any difference between them except the differing sound of the letters?

Ad.—I could not, nor do I think there is any difference.

Aug.—What if all things which are uttered by the articulate voice with some significance are both words and nouns, but yet words for one reason and nouns for another. Will there be any difference between a noun and a word?

Ad.—I do not understand how.

Aug.—You understand this at least, namely, that everything colored is visible, and everything visible is colored, although the two words signify distinctly and differently.

Ad.—I do understand it.

Aug.—Well now, how will it be, if in this way every word is a noun and every noun is a word, although these two nouns, or two words, namely, *noun* and *word,* have different significations?

Ad.—I now see that this can happen. But I want you to explain to me how it happens.

Aug.—You observe, I think, that everything which is expressed by the articulate voice with some signification both strikes the ear so that it can be sensed and is committed to memory so that it can be known.

Ad.—I do observe it.

Aug.—Then two things happen when we utter something in that sort of voice.

Ad.—That is so.

Aug.—What if words be called such because of one fact and names be called names because of another, that is, words [*verba*] from the striking [*a verberando*] and nouns from the knowing [*a noscendo*]? As the first is called such with regard to the ears, should not the second be called such in reference to the soul?

13. Ad.—I shall agree when you have shown how all words may correctly be called nouns.

Aug.—That is easy. For I believe that you agree that a pronoun is so called because it stands for a noun and yet denotes a thing with less complete signification than does the noun. For I think that the rule you learned in grammar gave the definition thus: A pronoun is a part of speech which when put in place of a noun signifies the same thing, although less fully.

Ad.—I remember and I agree.

Aug.—You see, therefore, that according to this definition pronouns serve only nouns and can be substituted in place of these alone, as when we say: "this man, the ruler himself, the same woman, this gold, that silver." *This, himself, same, this, that* are pronouns. *Man, king, woman, gold,* and *silver* are nouns by which things are signified more fully than by pronouns.

Ad.—I see and agree.

Aug.—Now mention a few conjunctions, such as you please.

Ad.—*Et, que, at,* and *atque.*

Aug.—Do not all these things which you have expressed seem to you to be nouns?

Ad.—Not exactly.

Aug.—Did I not speak correctly when I said: "all these things which you have expressed"?

Ad.—Quite correctly. And I see with admiration that you have shown that I did express nouns, for otherwise the statement "all these things" could not have been said of them correctly. But still I fear you seem to me to speak correctly because I do not deny that the four conjunctions are words, so that "all these things" could be said of them correctly because "all these words" is said correctly. But if you ask me what part of speech *words* is, I can only say "noun." So that perhaps the pronoun modifies this noun, and thus your statement is correct.

14. Aug.—Indeed you are acutely mistaken. But in order that you may no longer be deceived, attend more closely to what I say, if indeed I am able to say it as I wish. For discussing words with words is as entangled as interlocking and rubbing the fingers with the fingers, in which case it may scarcely be distinguished, except by the one himself who does it, which fingers itch and which give aid to the itching.

Ad.—Your example has indeed aroused my sharpest attention.

Aug.—Surely I pronounce words, and they consist in letters.

Ad.—That is so.

Aug.—And so, in the first place, in order that we may use that authority which is quite dear to us, when the Apostle Paul said, "Non erat in Christo Est et Non, sed Est in illo erat" [8] ["There was not in Christ yea and nay, but in Him was yea"], I

[8] II Corinthians I, 19.

do not think that we should consider that the three letters which we express when we say "Est" were in Christ, but rather that which is signified by these three letters.

Ad.—That is true.

Aug.—You understand, therefore, that he who said, "Est in illo erat" said only that that which is in Him is called "Est." Similarly, if he had said, "Virtus in illo erat" ("Virtue was in Him"), he would be understood to have said only that what is in Him is called virtue, nor should we think that the two syllables expressed in saying "virtue" were in Him and not that which was signified by the two syllables.

Ad.—I understand and follow.

Aug.—Do you not also understand that it makes no difference whether one says "is called virtue" or "is named virtue"?

Ad.—It is obvious.

Aug.—Hence it is obvious in the same way that it makes no difference whether one says, "That which is in Him is called *Est*" or "That which is in Him is named *Est.*"

Ad.—I see also that this makes no difference.

Aug.—Do you now see what I wish to show you?

Ad.—Not yet well enough.

Aug.—But you do see that a noun [name] is that by which something is called.

Ad.—That is very clear.

Aug.—Then you see that *Est* is a noun, if that which was in Him is named *Est.*

Ad.—I cannot deny it.

Aug.—And if I should ask you what part of speech, *Est* is, I think you would not say it is a noun [name] but a verb, although you have learned by reasoning that it is also a noun.

Ad.—That is exactly what I should say.

Aug.—Do you still doubt that other parts of speech are also nouns in the same way as has been shown?

Ad.—I do not doubt it, since I admit that they signify some-thing. But if you ask what each one of the things which they signify is called or named, I can but answer those very parts of speech which we do not call nouns [names], but which are shown to be so called.

15. Aug.—Are you not at all disquieted lest there be someone who might weaken this reasoning of ours by saying that power over things should be ascribed to the Apostle, but not power over words, and that, therefore, the foundation of this state-ment is not as firm as we think; that it is possible that although Paul lived and taught with rectitude, yet that he spoke in-correctly when he said, "Est in illo erat," [9] especially since he confessed that he was unskilled in speaking? How then could this be refuted?

Ad.—I have no objection to make, and I beg you to find someone whose prestige is recognized among those who are skilled in words, that by his authority you may more ably effect what you wish.

Aug.—Indeed, because authority is lacking does that reason-ing seem less qualified by means of which we have shown that something is signified by every part of speech, and if signified, then called; if called, then named; if named, then surely named by a noun [name]. This can be easily determined by consider-ing different languages. For anyone can see that if you ask what the Greeks call what we call *quis* [who], the answer is τίς; what the Greeks call what we call *volo* [I fly], the answer is θέλω; what the Greeks call what we call *bene* [well], the answer is καλῶς; what the Greeks call what we call *scriptum* [text], the answer is τὸ γεγραμμένον; what the Greeks call what we call *et* [and], the answer is καί; what the Greeks call what we call *ab* [from], the answer is ἀπό; what the Greeks call what we call *heu* [alas], the answer is οἴ. And it seems that he who

[9] II Corinthians, XI, 6.

thus asks speaks correctly, which would not be possible unless the above parts of speech were nouns. And so since we can maintain that Paul spoke correctly, even if the authority of all orators be absent, why is there need to look for some individual by whom our decision may be substantiated?

16. But some duller or less cautious person might not grant this, and might assert that it ought not to be granted without the authority of those who are by general consensus guardians of the rules of words; hence I ask, can there be anyone available who excels in the Latin language more than Cicero? But he, in those superb orations of his named Verrine, called the preposition *coram* (or in this case it may be an adverb) a noun. And yet since it is possible that I do not understand this context well enough and that it can be explained in different ways either by myself or by another, it is, I think, a thing to which no answer may be made. Now the noble masters of argument teach that a complete sentence is made up of a noun and a verb, which may be either affirmed or denied. Tullius in one place calls this a proposition. And when it is the third person of the verb, they say that the nominative case of the noun should accompany it, which is true, for if you consider with me as we say "homo sedet" [the man sits], "equus currit" [the horse runs], you will agree, I think, that they are two propositions.

Ad.—I do acknowledge that.

Aug.—You see there is a noun in each: in the first, *man,* and in the second, *horse;* and there is a verb in each: in the first, *sits,* and in the second, *runs.*

Ad.—I do see.

Aug.—Then if I were to say "sits" only or "runs" only, you would rightly ask me "who" or "what," and I should answer "man," or "horse," or "animal" or anything else, by which the noun can be restored to the verb and the proposition be completed, that is, the sentence which can be affirmed or denied.

Ad.—I understand.

Aug.—But attend to the rest. Suppose we see something remote and are uncertain whether it be an animal or a stone or something else, and suppose I say to you: "Because it is a man, it is an animal." Would I not speak rashly?

Ad.—Quite rashly, though not at all if you said: "If it is a man, then it is an animal."

Aug.—That is true. And what pleases me in your statement is *si* [if]. It pleases you too. But the *because* in my statement dissatisfies both of us.

Ad.—I agree.

Aug.—Now see whether these two statements are complete propositions: *if* pleases, *because* displeases.

Ad.—They are.

Aug.—Tell me now which are the verbs and which the nouns in those propositions.

Ad.—I see that *pleases* and *displeases* are the verbs, but what except *if* and *because* are the nouns?

Aug.—Then it is sufficiently proved that the two conjunctions are also nouns?

Ad.—Quite sufficiently.

Aug.—Can you treat other parts of speech in such a way that they will fall under the same rule?

Ad.—I can.

CHAPTER VI

SIGNS WHICH SIGNIFY THEMSELVES

17. *Aug.*—Then let us move on. Tell me whether, as we have found that all words [*verba*] are nouns and all nouns are words [*verba*], all nouns seem to you to be *vocabula* [words] and all *vocabula* [words] nouns?

Ad.—Clearly, I do not see what difference there is between them except in the sound of the syllables.

Aug.—At present I raise no objection, although some make a distinction in regard to the meaning, but we need not consider their opinion now. You surely note, however, that we have now discovered those signs which mutually signify each other, differing only in sound, and which signify themselves as well as all the other parts of speech.

Ad.—I do not understand.

Aug.—Do you not understand that a noun is signified by *vocabulum* [a word] and *vocabulum* by a noun, and that thus there is no difference between them beyond the sound of the letters in so far as *noun* in the general sense is concerned; for we also say "noun" in that special sense in which it is one of the eight parts of speech, so that it does not contain the other seven.

Ad.—I understand.

Aug.—But this is what I said, namely, that *vocabulum* and *noun* mutually signify each other.

18. Ad.—I grasp that, but I ask why you said: "since they signify themselves as well as the other parts of speech"?

Aug.—Did not our reasoning teach us that all parts of speech can be called nouns and *vocabula,* that is, can be signified by both *noun* and *vocabula*?

Ad.—That is so.

Aug.—What about *noun* itself, that is, that sound expressed by the two syllables [*nomen*]? If I ask what you call it, will you not correctly answer me with "noun"?

Ad.—Yes.

Aug.—Does the sign which we express when we say the four syllables "conjunctio" [conjunction] signify itself in this way? For this noun cannot be numbered with those things which it signifies.

Ad.—I quite accept that.

Aug.—That is because it has been said that *noun* signifies itself along with the other things which it signifies, and this, you may discern for yourself, also holds for *vocabulum.*

Ad.—That is now easy. But it has just occurred to me that *noun* is said both in a general sense and in a special sense, yet I do not take *vocabulum* to be among the eight parts of speech. It seems to me, therefore, that they differ in this respect in addition to the difference of sound between them.

Aug.—Do you think that *noun* [*nomen:* name] and ὄνομα differ otherwise than by the sound through which the Latin and Greek languages are distinguished?

Ad.—Indeed that is just what I understand.

Aug.—Then we have discovered those signs which (1) signify themselves, and (2) of which each is signified reciprocally by the other; (3) whatever is signified by one is signified by the other, (4) sound being the only difference between them. Of these only the fourth is a new discovery; for the three former are understood of *noun* and of *word* [*verbum*].

Ad.—It is entirely clear.

<h3 style="text-align:center">CHAPTER VII</h3>

<h4 style="text-align:center">CONCLUSION OF THE PRECEDING CHAPTERS</h4>

19. Aug.—Now I wish to review what we have discovered by means of this discussion.

Ad.—I shall do it in so far as I can. I remember that first of all we asked for what reason we speak. And it was found that we speak for the sake of teaching or reminding, since when we question we only do it that he who is asked may learn what we wish to hear; and that singing, which we seem to do for pleasure, is not properly speaking; that in praying to God whom we cannot suppose to be taught or reminded, words are for the purpose either of reminding ourselves or that others may be taught or reminded through us. Then, when it was clearly understood that words are only signs, you quoted a line in order that I might show what each word signified. And the line was: *Si nihil ex tanta superis placet urbe relinqui.* Although the second word was quite well known and very obvious, still I could not find what it means. And since it seemed to me that it is not used fecklessly in discourse, but that we use it in order to teach something by it to the hearer, you suggested that perhaps this word indicates an affection of the mind in which the mind seeks something and finds, or thinks it finds, that the something does not exist. Then, avoiding with a jest deep matters unknown to me, you put off the explanation until another time; and do not think that I have forgotten that you owe it me also. Then, when I was overtaxed to explain the third word in the line, you urged me not to substitute another word with the same meaning, but rather to indicate the thing itself which is signified by means of the word. And when we understood that this cannot be done in the act of speaking, we came to those things which are shown to the questioner by pointing the finger. I thought that these included all corporeal things, but we found that they are only the visible things. From here we went on, I do not know just how, to deaf men and actors who signify by gesture and without the use of words, not only things which can be seen, but also many others and almost everything that we say. Still we found that gestures themselves are signs. Then again we began to inquire how we can show without any signs the things themselves which are signified by the signs; since *wall,* and *color,* and everything visible that is shown by pointing the finger were all proved to be shown by a certain sign. I erred in having said that nothing of this sort could be found, and at length we agreed that those things can be shown without a sign, which we are not in the act of doing when we are asked about them and which we can do after being asked. But speaking does not belong to this genus. For if, while we are in the act of speaking, we are asked what speaking is, it is quite evident that it is easy to show it by means of itself.

20. By this we were reminded that either signs show signs, or they show other things which are not signs, or else without a sign are shown things which we can do after we are questioned. And we undertook to investigate and discuss the first of these three more thoroughly. In this discussion it was revealed that the signs are in part those which cannot in turn be signified by means of those signs which they signify, as in the four-syllable word *conjunctio* [conjunction]; in part, the signs are those which can in turn be signified by means of those signs which they signify, as when we say "sign," we also signify *word* [*verbum*], and when we say "word" we also signify *sign;* for *sign* and *word* are both two signs and two words. It was shown, moreover, that in this genus in which signs signify each other mutually, some mean not as much, some mean just as much, and some mean exactly the same thing. For the two-syllable word *sign* [*signum*] signifies absolutely everything by means of which anything is signified. *Word* [*verbum*] is not, however, a sign of all signs, but only of those which are uttered by the articulate voice; consequently, it is clear that although *word* [*verbum*] is signified by *sign* [*signum*] and *sign* by *word,* namely, the two former syllables by the latter two and the latter two by the former two, yet *sign* [*signum*] means more than *word* [*verbum*], for more things are signified by the former two syllables than by the latter two. But *word* in general means just as much as *noun* in general. For our reasoning taught us that all parts of speech are also nouns; for pronouns

can be added to them, and it can be said of all that they name something; and there is none of them which cannot make a complete proposition when a verb is added to it. But although *word* [*verbum*] and *noun* [*nomen*] mean just the same amount because all things which are words are also names, yet they do not mean the same thing. It was argued, and with sufficient reason, that things are called words for one reason and nouns for another, since the former were found to be impressed on the vibration of the ear, but the latter on the memory of the mind; and this can be understood from the fact that in talking we correctly say "What is the name of this thing?" when we wish to commit it to memory, whereas we do not say "What is the word of this thing?" We found that *noun* and ὄνομα signify not only just as much but also the same thing exactly, and there is no difference between them except that of the differing sound in the letters. I had forgotten that in the genus in which signs signify each other mutually, we found no sign which does not signify itself as well as the other things which it signifies. I have recalled these things as best I could. Do you now, whom I believe to have spoken always with knowledge and certainty in this discussion, see whether I have set forth these things well and in good order.

CHAPTER VIII

THESE ARGUMENTS ARE NOT IN VAIN. LIKEWISE, WHEN SIGNS ARE HEARD, THE MIND MUST BE DIRECTED TOWARDS THE THINGS WHICH ARE SIGNIFIED, IN ORDER THAT THE QUESTIONER MAY BE ANSWERED

21. *Aug.*—You have recalled adequately all the things which I wanted, and now I acknowledge to you that these distinctions

seem much clearer to me than they were when we unearthed them from unknown hiding places. But it is difficult at this point to say just where I am striving to lead you by so many circumlocutions. For it may seem that we are quibbling and so diverting the mind from earnest matters with naïve questions, or that we are seeking after some mean advantage. Or, if you suspect that this investigation tends towards some worthy object, you desire to know now what it is we strive after or at least you want it to be mentioned. But I want you to believe that I wish neither to have occupied myself with quibbles in this discussion, although we can afford to pun if the matter is not viewed naïvely; nor to have labored for petty or unimportant ends. Still if I say that there is a blessed life, to which I desire that we may be led under God's guidance, that is, by truth itself through stages of a degree suited to our weak progress, I fear to appear laughable because I have set out on such a road by considering not the things themselves which are signified, but signs. But be indulgent with this preparation, since it is not for amusement, but in order to exercise the strength and keenness of the mind by means of which we can not only bear the warmth and light of that region where the blessed life resides, but can also love the true.

Ad.—But do continue as you began, for I never think those things unimportant which you consider suitable to say or to do.

22. *Aug.*—Then come, and let us consider that case in which signs signify not other signs, but those things which we call signifiable. First, however, tell me whether a man is a man.

Ad.—But now you do seem to me to be jesting.

Aug.—Why so?

Ad.—Because you think that I should be asked whether man is anything other than man [*homo*].

Aug.—I believe that you would also think that you were

being bantered if I should ask whether the first syllable of this word be other than *ho* and the second other than *mo?*

Ad.—Indeed I should.

Aug.—But these two syllables conjoined are man [*homo*], or do you object?

Ad.—Who could object to that?

Aug.—Now I ask whether you are these two conjoined syllables.

Ad.—Not at all, but your purpose is clear.

Aug.—Then tell me, and do not think me abusive.

Ad.—I infer that you think that I am not a man [*homo*].

Aug.—Why did you not think the same when you granted the truth of all the former inferences, from which this is derived?

Ad.—I shall not tell you what I think until I first hear from you whether, when you asked if man is man [*homo*], you were asking about the two syllables or about the thing itself which they signify.

Aug.—Do you rather tell me in what reference you take my questions; for if the reference is ambiguous you should have taken care not to answer me before making certain how I put the question.

Ad.—But how could the equivocation embarrass me, when I have answered both: for man is absolutely man [*homo*], and the two syllables are only the two syllables, and that which they signify is nothing other than that which it is.

Aug.—Of course you know this. But why have you only construed the word *homo* in two ways, and not also the other words which we have spoken?

Ad.—I am not at all certain that the others should not have been construed in this way.

Aug.—If you had construed my first question, not to mention the others, entirely in the sense in which the syllables sound, you would have made no answer, for I could not have seemed to ask anything. But just now when I pronounced the three words, one of which I reiterated in the center, saying "utrum homo homo sit" [whether man is man], you did not construe the first and last words as signs, but according to the things which are signified by them, and this is evident from the fact that you thought at once with certainty and confidence that my question should be answered.

Ad.—That is true.

Aug.—Then why did it seem suitable to you to construe the one I repeated both according to the way in which it sounded and according to the thing which it signified?

Ad.—Ah, well, I now construe it entirely in the sense in which something is signified, for I do agree with you that we cannot discuss at all unless when we hear words we direct the mind to the things of which they are the signs. So now show me how that inference deceived me so that I concluded that I am not a man.

Aug.—No; rather, I shall question you again in order that you may discover your error.

Ad.—Excellent.

23. *Aug.*—I shall not ask over again my first questions, for you have answered those already. Now, consider more carefully whether the syllable *ho* in *homo* is only the syllable *ho* and whether *mo* is only *mo*.

Ad.—I do not see any difference.

Aug.—See whether *homo* is not made by joining *ho* and *mo*.

Ad.—I do not agree at all. For we decided, and rightly so, when a sign is expressed to attend to that which is signified, and from the consideration of that to deny or affirm what is said. It has also been granted that, since the syllables uttered separately are expressed without any signification, they are just as they sound.

Aug.—It is agreed then and firmly established in your mind that answers ought to be made only to questions which are about things which are signified by words.

Ad.—It seems to me agreeable if the words are only words.

Aug.—Very well, but how would you refute that sophist of whom we hear, who asserted that when his opponent spoke a lion issued from his mouth? For first the sophist asked whether what we express proceeds from the mouth, which his opponent could not deny. Next he manipulated the conversation, which was easily done, so that his opponent pronounced "lion" in speaking. And when his opponent had done this, the sophist began to badger and heckle him, because his opponent had admitted that whatever we say comes forth from the mouth; nor was his opponent able to deny that he had spoken "lion," and the sophist asked the tormented victim if he who were seen to vomit such an enormous beast were not an evil fellow.

Ad.—It would be quite easy to refute this quibbler, for I should not admit that whatever we say proceeds from our mouth. For what we say we signify; and, in speaking, what issues from the mouth is not the thing itself which is signified, but the sign by means of which it is signified, except in that case in which signs themselves are signified, a genus which we previously discussed.

24. *Aug.*—Ah, in this way you would have held your own against him. Nevertheless, what will you say when I ask whether *man* is a noun?

Ad.—What indeed, but that it is a noun?

Aug.—And when I look at you do I see a noun?

Ad.—No.

Aug.—Do you wish me to say what follows?

Ad.—No, not at all, for I can answer myself that I am not that man which I have called a noun when you ask whether *man* is a noun; for it has been agreed that we are to affirm or to deny what is said according to the thing which is signified.

Aug.—But it seems to me not merely incidental that you made that answer, for your discrimination was ruled by the law of reason itself which has been placed within our minds. For if I should ask what man is, you would perhaps answer that he is an animal. But if I were to ask what part of speech *man* is, you could answer correctly only a noun. Accordingly, when *man* is found to be both a noun and an animal, the former is said in the sense in which it is a sign, the latter is said in the sense of the thing which is signified. And so when anyone asks whether *man* is a noun, I can only answer that it is, for the question thus put indicates clearly that the questioner wishes to be answered according to the sense in which *man* is a sign. But if he asks whether man is an animal, I may assent much more readily, since if he asked only what man is and indicated nothing in regard to *man* and to *animal,* my mind would fix itself according to the law of speaking towards that which is signified by the two syllables *homo* [man], and the answer would be "animal" only, or I might even give the full definition, namely, a rational, mortal animal. Do you understand the matter in this way?

Ad.—I do entirely. But when we have granted that *man* is a noun, how shall we avoid that absurd conclusion by which we are asserted not to be men?

Aug.—How indeed except by pointing out that the conclusion does not follow from the sense in which we agreed with the questioner? Or if he confesses to mean it not as a thing-reference but as a sign-reference, we need not be apprehensive, for why should one fear to admit that he is not a man [*homo*], namely, that he is not made up of three syllables.

Ad.—Very true. Why then is it offensive to us when it is said: "You, therefore, are not man [*homo*]," since according to our discussion that is quite true?

Aug.—Because one cannot help thinking that the conclusion bears a reference to that which is signified by the two syllables *homo* [man] as soon as the words are expressed, by virtue of that law which by nature is very strong, namely, that when signs are heard the attention is turned towards the things signified.

Ad.—I accept what you say.

CHAPTER IX

WHETHER ALL THINGS, AND ALSO THE COGNITION OF THEM, SHOULD
BE PREFERRED TO THEIR SIGNS

25. *Aug.*—Now then, I wish you to understand that things which are signified are more to be depended upon than signs. For whatever exists because of another must of necessity be inferior to that because of which it exists, unless you think otherwise.

Ad.—It seems to me that assent should not be given too hastily. For when we say *coenum* [filth], this noun, I think, is far superior to that which it signifies. What offends us when we hear it does not pertain to the sound of the word itself, since *coenum* [filth] is changed by a single letter from *coelum* [heaven]. But we do see what a great difference there is between the things signified by these nouns. Hence I should not attribute to this sign what we so loathe in the thing signified. So for this reason I consider the sign superior to the thing, for we hear the sign with greater complaisance than we perceive the thing by means of any sense.

Aug.—Most watchful indeed. It is false, therefore, that all things are to be considered superior to their signs?

Ad.—It seems so.

Aug.—Then tell me what plan you think they followed who gave a name to this vile and despicable thing [*coenum:* filth]. Do you approve of them or not?

Ad.—Indeed, how should I dare to approve or to disapprove, for I do not know what plan they followed?

Aug.—At least you can determine what plan you follow when you utter the name.

Ad.—Clearly I can; for I wish to signify that which I think ought to be taught or reminded in order to teach or to remind him with whom I am speaking of the thing itself.

Aug.—The teaching or reminding, or the being taught or being reminded, which you either express suitably by means of the name or which is expressed to you—ought that not to be held superior to the name itself?

Ad.—I grant that the knowledge itself which results from the sign should be considered superior to the sign, but not for that reason, I think, the thing also.

26. *Aug.*—In this argument of ours, therefore, although it be false that all things ought to be considered superior to their signs, yet it is not false that everything which exists because of another is inferior to that because of which it exists. Surely, the cognition of filth because of which the noun [name] *filth* was determined ought to be considered superior to the noun itself which we found to be superior to filth itself. For the cognition is considered superior to the sign of which we spoke for the sole reason that it is proved conclusively that the sign exists because of the cognition and not the cognition because of the sign. Since, for example, when a certain glutton and servant of the belly, as the Apostle calls him,[10] said that he lived in order to eat, the temperate man who heard him chided him and said: "Would it not be better to eat in order to live?" This was clearly said in conformity with the rule that inferiors exist

10 Romans, XVI, 18.

for the sake of superiors. And the Apostle was displeased only because the glutton's life should be of so little worth to him that he would have it degraded by the passion of gluttony as indicated by his saying that he lived for the sake of feasting. And this should be praised because the Apostle taught in these two distinctions that what ought to be done for the sake of something is that which should be subject to it, for it is understood that it is preferable to eat in order to live. Similarly you as well as other men who judge matters suitably would reply to a garrulous word-lover who said: "I teach in order to talk" with "Man, why not rather speak in order to teach?" For if these things are true, as you know they are, you truly see how much less words are to be esteemed than that for the sake of which we use words, since the use of words is superior to the words. For words exist in order that they may be used, and in addition we use them in order to teach. As teaching is superior to talking, in like degree speech is better than words. So of course doctrine is far superior to words. But I wish to hear whatever objections you have to offer.

27. *Ad.*—I agree indeed that doctrine is superior to words. But whether the rule that everything which exists for the sake of something else is inferior to that for the sake of which it exists has no exceptions is more than I am able to say.

Aug.—We shall discuss that more conveniently and more thoroughly at another time. For the present what you have granted is enough to prove what I now wish. For you grant that the cognition of things is superior to the signs of things. Consequently, the cognition of things which are signified is to be preferred to the cognition of signs by means of which they are signified. Do you agree?

Ad.—Did I admit that the cognition of things is superior to the cognition of signs, and not just to signs themselves? Then I fear that I am not in agreement with you on this point. For if *coenum* [filth], the noun [name], is better than the thing it signifies, then the cognition of the noun [name] ought also to be preferred to the cognition of the thing, although the noun itself be inferior to the cognition. Indeed there are four considerations involved: (1) the noun, (2) the thing, (3) the cognition of the noun, (4) the cognition of the thing. Since the first is more excellent than the second, why is not the third better than the fourth? But if it is not better, must it therefore be considered as inferior?

28. *Aug.*—I see that you have very admirably retained what you conceded and understood what you thought. But you understand, I think, that the three-syllable word *vitium* [vice] is better than that which it signifies, though the cognition of the noun itself is far inferior to the knowledge of vices. Granted that you thus arrange and consider the four distinctions: (1) noun, (2) thing, (3) cognition of noun, (4) cognition of thing, we correctly place the first before the second. For the noun placed in the verse where Persius says,[11] "But he is drunk with vice," not only does not vitiate the verse but adds a certain ornament. But when the thing itself which is signified by this noun [*vitium*] is in anything it does vitiate it. So thus we see that the third does not excel the fourth, but the fourth the third. For the cognition of the noun *vitium* [vice] exists for the sake of the cognition [knowledge] of vices.

Ad.—Do you think that the cognition of vices is preferable even though it makes men more wretched? For among all the afflictions which man suffers, devised by the cruelty or cupidity of tyrants, this same Persius ranks first that torture which re-results when men are forced to acknowledge vices which they cannot avoid.

Aug.—Reasoning in this way, you can also deny that a knowledge [cognition] of virtues is preferable to the cognition

[11] *Satyra*, 3, v. 33.

of the word *virtue*. Because to see virtue but not to possess it is torture, and it was by this means that the satirist wished tyrants to be punished.[12]

Ad.—May God avert such madness. Now I do see that knowledge [the cognitions themselves] by which learning instructs the soul is not to be held as culpable, but that those men are to be judged the most pitiable of all, as I think Persius judged them, who are infected by such a malady that there is no remedy for it.

Aug.—You understand quite well. But then of what real moment is the opinion of Persius, the satirist, since in problems of the sort before us we are not subject to the authority of satirists? Well, if in some way one cognition is to be preferred to another, still that point is not easily explained just now. I am satisfied that it has been shown that the cognition of the thing which a sign signifies is more powerful than the sign itself, even if it is not superior to the cognition of a sign. Hence, let us discuss more thoroughly what the genus is of those things which we said can be shown through themselves [*per se*] without signs, as speaking, walking, sitting, throwing, etc.

Ad.—I recall now what you speak of.

CHAPTER X

WHETHER CERTAIN THINGS CAN BE TAUGHT WITHOUT SIGNS.
THINGS ARE NOT LEARNED THROUGH WORDS THEMSELVES.

29. *Aug.*—Does it seem to you that anything which may be immediately done when one asks a question about it can be shown without a sign, or do you see some exception?

Ad.—Running through the items of this whole genus time

12 *Satyra*, 3, v. 35-38.

and again, I do not indeed find anything in it which can be taught without some sign, except perhaps speaking and also possibly teaching. For I see that whatever I do after his question in order that he may learn, the questioner does not learn from the thing itself which he desires to have shown him. For if I am asked what walking is when I am still, or doing something else, and if I, by walking immediately, try to teach without a sign what has been asked—all of which has been discussed earlier— then how shall I avoid having the asker think that walking consists in walking only so far as I walked? And if he did think that he would be misinformed, for if someone walked not so far or farther than I did the questioner would think that this individual had not walked. And what I have said about this one word will be true of all the others which we thought could be shown without a sign, except the ones we excluded (talking and teaching).

30. Aug.—I accept that, in truth; but does it not seem to you that speaking is one thing and teaching another?

Ad.—Surely it does, for if they were the same, none would teach without speaking, and since we teach many things by means of signs which are not words, who can doubt there is a difference?

Aug.—Are teaching and signifying the same or do they differ in some way?

Ad.—I think that they are the same.

Aug.—Is it not true that we signify in order to teach?

Ad.—That is true.

Aug.—What if it be said that we teach in order to signify? Is the assertion not easily refuted by the former statement?

Ad.—That is so.

Aug.—If then we signify that we may teach and do not teach in order to signify, teaching is one thing, signifying another.

Ad.—That is true, nor did I answer correctly that both are the same.

Aug.—Now tell me if he who teaches what teaching is does it by signifying or in some other way.

Ad.—I do not see that there is any other way.

Aug.—Therefore, what you said awhile ago is false, namely, that when someone asks what teaching is the thing itself can be taught without signs, since we see that not even this can be done without signifying. For you have granted that signifying is one thing, teaching another. And if, as it seems, they are different, and teaching is only by means of signifying, then teaching is not shown through itself [*per se*], as you thought. Consequently, nothing has yet been found which can be shown through itself except speaking which also signifies itself as well as other things. Yet since this is a sign also it is still not entirely clear what things can be taught without the aid of signs.

Ad.—I have no reason for disagreeing with you.

31. Aug.—It has been proved, therefore, that nothing is taught without signs, and that cognition itself should be dearer to us than the signs by means of which we cognize, although all things which are signified cannot be greater than their signs.

Ad.—It seems so.

Aug.—Do you recall by what great circumlocutions we at length reached this slight point? For since we began this interchange of words which has occupied us for some time, we have labored to discover the following three points: 1. whether anything can be taught without signs, 2. whether certain signs ought to be preferred to the things which they signify, 3. whether the cognition of things is superior to their signs. But there is a fourth point which I wish to know briefly from you, namely, whether you think that these points are so clear and distinct that you cannot doubt them.

Ad.—I wish indeed to have arrived at certainty after such

great doubts and complications, but your question disturbs me, although I do not know why, and keeps me from agreeing. For I see that you would not have asked me about this, if you did not have some objection to raise, and the problem is such a labyrinth that I am not able to explore it thoroughly or to answer with assurance, for I am disquieted lest something lie hidden in these windings which evades the keenness of my mind.

Aug.—I commend your hesitation. For it indicates a mind which is cautious and this is the greatest safeguard to equanimity. It is very difficult not to be perturbed when things we consider easily and readily provable are shaken by contrary arguments and, as it were, are wrenched from our hands. For just as it is proper to assent to things well explored and perused, so it is perilous to consider things known which are not known. Because there is a danger, when those things are often upset which we supposed would stand firmly and endure, lest we fall into such distrust and hatred of reason that it might seem that confidence in evident truth itself is not warranted.

32. But come, let us consider more diligently whether you think any of the points should be doubted. For consider, if someone unskilled in the art of bird-catching, which is done with reeds and bird-lime, should happen upon a fowler, carrying his instruments as he walked along though not fowling at the time, he would hasten to follow and in wonderment he would reflect and ask himself, as indeed he might, what the man's equipment meant. Now if the fowler, seeing himself watched, were to exhibit his art, and skilfully employ the reed, and then noting a little bird nearby, if he were to charm, approach, and capture it with his reed and hawk, would the fowler not teach his observer without the use of signification, but rather by means of the thing itself which the observer desired to know?

Ad.—I fear this observer of bird-catching is like the man whom I referred to above, who inquires about walking; for it does not seem that in this case the entire art of fowling is exhibited.

Aug.—It is easy to free you from that worry. For I suggest that an observer might be intelligent enough to recognize the whole complexity of the art from what he saw. It is enough for our purpose if certain men can be taught without signs about some things, if indeed not about all things.

Ad.—To that I can add that if the learner be very intelligent he will know what walking is fully when it has been shown by a few steps.

Aug.—That is agreeable. And I not only do not object, but I approve of your statement. For you see that the conclusion has been reached by both of us, namely, that some men can be taught certain things without signs, and that what we thought awhile back is false, that is, that there is nothing at all which can be shown without signs. For now of that sort, not one thing only or another, but thousands of things occur to the mind, which may be shown through themselves when no sign has been given. Why then do we hesitate, I pray you? For passing over the innumerable spectacles of men in every theater where things are shown through themselves without signs, surely the sun and this light bathing and clothing all things, the moon and the other stars, the lands and the seas, and all things which are generated in them without number, are all exhibited and shown through themselves by God and nature to those who perceive them.

33. If we consider this more carefully, then perhaps you may find that there is nothing which is learned by means of signs. For when a sign is given me, if it finds me not knowing of what thing it is a sign, it can teach me nothing, but if it finds me knowing the thing of which it is the sign, what do I learn

from the sign? For the word does not show me the thing which it signifies when I read: *Et saraballae eorum non sunt immutatae* [13] (And their *saraballae* are not changed). For if head-coverings of some sort are called by this name [*saraballae*], when I have heard it have I learned either what a head is or what coverings are? I knew these before, and it is not when someone names them, but when they are seen by me that knowledge of them is achieved for me. And indeed when the two syllables "caput" [head] were first expressed to me, I knew as little what they meant as when I first heard or read *saraballae*. But when "caput" was repeated over and over, as I observed and noticed when it was said, I found it to be the word of a thing which was already well known to me by sight. Before I discovered this the word was only a sound to me, and I learned that it is a sign when I found out of what thing it is a sign; which thing, indeed, I had learned, as I said above, not through its signification but by the sight of it. Therefore that the sign is learned after the thing is cognized is rather more the case than that the thing itself is learned after the sign is given.

34. That you may understand this more exactly, let us suppose that we now hear for the first time the word "caput" [head], and not knowing whether it is merely a meaningless sound or whether something is signified, we ask what "caput" [head] is. (Remember we want to have knowledge of the sign itself and not of the thing which it signifies, which knowledge we certainly lack as long as we do not know of what it is a sign.) And if, when we inquire, the thing itself is shown us by means of pointing the finger, when we have seen the thing we learn the sign which we had only heard before without knowing it. Since, however, two factors are involved with the sign, namely, sound and signification, we surely perceive the sound not through the sign but through the vibration when the

[13] Daniel, III, 94.

ear is struck, while we learn the signification when the thing itself is shown. For the pointing of the finger can signify only that towards which the finger is pointed, but it was pointed not at the sign but at the member which is called the head; consequently, I have not learned by means of the pointing what the thing is, for I knew that already, nor did I learn the sign in that way since the pointing was not directed at the sign. But I do not wish to place too much emphasis on the pointing of the finger, because it seems to me that it is rather a sign of the demonstration itself rather than of the things demonstrated; as in the case of the adverb *ecce* [behold], for we are accustomed to point the finger with this adverb lest one sign of demonstration be not enough. And if I can, I shall try to prove to you above all that we learn nothing through those signs which are termed words. For it is more correct, as I have said, that we learn the meaning of the word, that is, the signification which is hidden in the sound when the thing itself which it signifies has been cognized, than that we perceive the thing through such signification.

35. And what I have said about *head,* I should say, too, of *coverings* [clothes] and of innumerable other things. And though I already know these, yet *saraballae* I do not know in the least. If someone were to indicate them by gesture or sketch them for me or show me something to which they are similar, I do not say that he would not teach me (which I could maintain if I wished to speak a little more fully). But I do say what is quite relevant to the point being discussed, namely, that he would not have taught me by means of words. If someone, seeing these *saraballae* while I was near, should bring them to my attention, saying "Ecce saraballas" [Here are the head-coverings], I would learn something unknown, not through the words which were spoken, but through its appearance, by means of which I was made to know and to retain the mean-

ing of the name. For when I learned the thing itself I was not indebted to the words of others but to my eyes; yet perhaps I accepted their words in order to attend, that is, in order that I might find what was to be seen.

CHAPTER XI

WE DO NOT LEARN THROUGH THE WORDS WHICH SOUND
OUTWARDLY, BUT THROUGH THE TRUTH
WHICH TEACHES WITHIN US

36. To give them as much credit as possible, words possess only sufficient efficacy to remind us in order that we may seek things, but not to exhibit the things so that we may know them. He teaches me something, moreover, who presents to my eyes or to any other bodily sense or even to my mind itself those things which I wish to know. By means of words, therefore, we learn only words or rather the sound and vibration of words, for if those things which are not signs cannot be words, even though I have heard a word, I do not know that it is a word until I know what it signifies. So when things are known the cognition of the words is also accomplished, but by means of hearing words they are not learned. For we do not learn the words which we know, nor can we say that we learn those which we do not know unless their signification has been perceived; and this happens not by means of hearing words which are pronounced, but by means of a cognition of the things which are signified. For it is the truest reasoning and most correctly said that when words are uttered we either know already what they signify or we do not know; if we know, then we remember rather than learn, but if we do not know, then we do not even remember, though perhaps we are prompted to ask.

37. If you say this, we cannot know the head-coverings, the name of which is only a sound to us, unless we see them; and we cannot know the name itself more fully except by cognizing the things themselves. But we do accept the story of the boys, that they triumphed over the king and over the fires by faith and religion, that they sang praises to God, and that they won honor even from their very enemies. Has this been transmitted to us otherwise than by means of words? I answer that everything signified by these words was already in our knowledge. For I already grasp what three boys are, what a furnace is, and fire, and a king, what unhurt by fire is, and every thing else signified by those words. But Ananias and Azarias and Misael are as unknown to me as *saraballae;* these names do not help me at all to know these men, nor can they help me. I confess, moreover, that I believe rather than know that the things written in those stories were done at that time as they have been written; and those whom we believe knew the difference between believing and knowing. For the Prophet says: "If ye will not believe, ye shall not understand." [14] Surely he would not have said that, had he not thought that believing and understanding are different. Therefore, what I understand I also believe, but I do not understand everything that I believe; for all which I understand I know, but I do not know all that I believe. But still I am not unmindful of the utility of believing many things which are not known. I include in this utility the story about the three youths. And though the majority of things must remain unknown to me, yet I do know what is the utility of believing.

38. But, referring now to all things which we understand, we consult, not the speaker who utters words, but the guardian truth within the mind itself, because we have perhaps been reminded by words to do so. Moreover, He who is consulted

[14] Isaias, VII, 9.

teaches; for He who is said to reside in the interior man is Christ,[15] that is, the unchangeable excellence of God and His everlasting wisdom, which every rational soul does indeed consult. But there is revealed to each one as much as he can apprehend through his will according as it is more perfect or less perfect. And if sometimes one is deceived this is not due to a defect in the truth which he has consulted any more than it is a defect of external light that the eyes of the body are often deceived; yet we confess that we consult this external light about visible things in order that it may show them to us in so far as we have the power to discern.

CHAPTER XII

CHRIST THE TRUTH TEACHES WITHIN

39. If we consult light concerning color and other things which we sense through the body; if we consult the elements of this world and those bodies which we sense; if we consult the senses themselves which the mind uses as interpreters in recognizing things of this sort; and if we also consult the interior truth by means of reason about things which are understood: what can be said to indicate that we learn anything by means of words beyond that sound which strikes the ear? For all things which we perceive are perceived either through a sense of the body or by means of the mind. We call the former sensibles, the latter intelligibles; or to speak in the manner of our authorities, the former are carnal, the latter spiritual. If we are questioned about sensibles, we answer if the things sensed are at hand, as when we are questioned while gazing at the new moon as to where or of what sort it is.

[15] Ephesians, III, 16, 17.

If the one who questions does not see, he believes words, and often he does not believe; but he learns nothing unless he also sees what is mentioned. If he does learn, he learns by means of the things themselves and from his own senses, but not through the articulated words. For the same words are heard by the man who sees and by the man who does not see. But if a question is not about things immediately sensed, although it is about things which we have sensed in the past, in this case we speak not of things themselves but of images impressed by things on the mind and committed to memory. I do not in the least know how we can speak of these as true when we see that they are false, unless it is because we do not speak of what we see or what we sense, but of what we have seen or have sensed. Thus we carry these images in the recesses of the memory as documents of things sensed before. Contemplating these in the mind, we say nothing that is false if we speak with good conscience. But these documents are our own, and he who hears of them, if he has been in their presence and sensed them, learns nothing from my words, but rather remembers [and confirms] what is said through the images hidden in himself. But if he has not perceived the things which are spoken of, it is clear that he believes [or accepts on trust] rather than learns through the words.

40. Indeed when things are discussed which we perceive through the mind, that is, by means of intellect and reason, these are said to be things which we see immediately in that interior light of truth by virtue of which he himself who is called the interior man is illumined, and upon this depends his joy. But then our hearer, if he also himself sees those things with his inner and pure eye, knows that of which I speak by means of his own contemplation, but not through my words. Accordingly, even though I speak about true things, I still do not teach him who beholds the true things, for he

is taught not through my words but by means of the things themselves which God reveals within the soul. Hence, if he is questioned, he can answer about these. What could be more absurd than to think that he is taught by means of my speaking, when even before I speak he can express those very things if questioned? Now, if it often happens that he who is questioned denies something, and is driven by other questions to affirm that which he denied, this happens because of a defect in his discrimination in so far as he cannot consult that light about the whole matter. He is advised to do it part by part when he is questioned by one step after another about those very parts of which the whole consists, which he is unable to grasp in its entirety. If he is guided in this case by the words of the questioner, still he does not accomplish the grasp of the whole by means of verbal instruction, but by means of questions put in such a way that he who is questioned is able to teach himself through his inner power according to the measure of his ability. An apt example is found in our recent procedure, for when I asked you whether anything can be taught by words, the question at first seemed absurd to you, because you did not have an inclusive view of the problem. Thus, it was suitable for me to formulate my questions in such a way that your powers might be brought under the direction of the inner teacher. Accordingly, I should say things which as I spoke you would admit to be true, of which you would be certain, and about which you would declare that you had knowledge. From what source would you learn these things? You would perhaps answer that I had taught them to you. To that I should reply: "What if I should say that I had seen a man flying?" Would my words carry the same certitude as if you should hear that wise men are superior to fools? You would immediately answer in the negative and assert that you do not believe the former statement, or if you do believe it, that you do not know it to be true, but that you do know the latter statement with great certainty. From this discussion you would understand clearly that you did not learn anything from me through words, neither about a man flying, of which you knew nothing though I did state it, nor about the relative worth of wise men and fools, which you did know quite well. If in addition you were also questioned about each word, you would state on oath that the latter is well known to you, while the former is not known. Then indeed you would admit all that you had denied, as you knew with clarity and certainty the things in which it consists. Whenever we say anything, either the hearer does not know whether what is said is false or true, or he knows that it is false, or he knows that it is true. In the first mode he will either believe (or accept in good confidence), or he will form an opinion, or he will hesitate; in the second mode he will resist the statement and reject it; in the third he merely confirms. In none of these three cases does the hearer learn anything from what is heard. For he who does not know about the thing after we have spoken, he who knows that what we said is false, and he who would be able upon being asked to state the same things without having heard them, are all three shown to have learned nothing through words.

CHAPTER XIII

THE POWER OF WORDS DOES NOT EVEN REVEAL THE MIND
OF THE SPEAKER

41. From what has been said it follows, therefore, that in the case of those things which are grasped by the mind, anyone who is unable to grasp them hears to no purpose the words of him

who does discern them; though we may make an exception in regard to the fact that where such things are unknown there is a certain utility in believing them until they are known. On the other hand, whoever can discern those things which are grasped by the mind is inwardly a pupil of truth and outwardly a judge of the speaker, or rather of his statements. For often he knows what has been said, though the speaker himself does not know; as if, for example, someone who is a follower of Epicurus and so thinks that the soul is mortal, should recite the arguments on the soul's immortality expounded by men of greater wisdom. If someone who is versed in spiritual things hears the speaker state the argument for the immortality of the soul, he will judge that true things have been said, but the speaker does not know that they are true; for, to the contrary, he thinks that they are quite false. Can he be understood as teaching what he does not know? He does use, however, the very same words which one who understood would use.

42. Now, therefore, not even this is left to words, namely, that at any rate they express the mind of the speaker, since a speaker may indeed not know the things about which he speaks. Consider also lying and deceiving, and you will easily understand from both of them that words not only do not disclose the true intention of the mind, but that they may serve to conceal it. For I by no means doubt that by words truthful men try, and to some extent do contrive, to disclose their minds, which would be accomplished, as all agree, if liars were not allowed to speak. And yet we have had the experience both in ourselves and in others of words being expressed which were not about the thing being thought. It seems to me that this can happen in two ways: (1) either when something which has been committed to memory and often repeated is expressed by one who is preoccupied with other things, as often happens to us when we

sing a hymn, (2) or when against our will we make a slip in speech, for in this case, too, signs are expressed which are not of the things which we have in mind. For indeed those who lie also think of the things which they express, so that, although we do not know whether they tell the truth, we do yet know that they have in mind what they are saying, if they do not do one of the two things cited above. If anyone contends that this only happens now and then, and is apparent when it happens, I do not object, though frequently it is not observed and has often deceived me.

43. But among these there is another genus of words, one which is very prevalent and the cause of countless disagreements and battles, namely, that which is involved when he who speaks signifies the thing which he is thinking, but for the most part only to himself and certain others, while he does not signify the same thing to the one to whom he speaks nor to some others. For should someone say in our presence that man is surpassed in manly power [*virtus*] by certain large animals, we should not be able to brook such a statement; and we should deny this false and repugnant assertion with vehemence, though perhaps the speaker meant by *manly power* bodily strength. He may have expressed by the word what he had in mind, neither lying, nor making a mistake about the thing, nor linking together memorized words while turning other things over in his mind, nor saying by a slip of the tongue what he did not intend to say. He merely calls the thing about which he was thinking by a name which is other than the one by which we call it. We should agree with him at once if we could read his mind and see directly the thought which he was unable to express by the words spoken and the statement made. They say that definition can cure this error, so that in this case, if the speaker were to define what virtue is, it would be clear that the controversy is

not about the thing but about the word. Now I may grant that this is so, but how often is it possible to find good definers? And yet many things have been charged against the science of defining, which are not approved by me in all respects, but it is not suitable to discuss this at present.

44. I pass over the fact that we hear many things imperfectly and yet wrangle long and forcefully as if we had heard perfectly; for example, you were saying but some time ago that you had heard that *piety* is signified by a certain Punic word which I had called *mercy,* and you had heard this from those who know the language well. But I objected and insisted that you had forgotten what you had heard, for you seemed to me to say "faith" rather than "piety," though you were sitting near me and the two words are by no means deceptive to the ear because of their similarity in sound. Yet for a long time I thought that you did not know what had been said to you, whereas it was I who did not know what you had said. If I had heard you well, it would not have seemed at all absurd to me that in Punic *piety* and *mercy* are called by one word. These things happen now and then, but, as I said, we shall overlook them lest I seem to bring false witness against words because of the negligence of the hearer or even because of human deafness. The points enumerated above are more distressing where, though we speak the same language as the speaker and the words are clearly heard and are Latin, we still are not able to understand the speaker.

45. But witness: I now relent and admit that when words are perceived in the hearing of him to whom they are known, the hearer may rest assured that the speaker has thought about the things which they signify. But we are now asking if for that reason he learns whether the speaker has told the truth?

CHAPTER XIV

CHRIST TEACHES WITHIN. MAN REMINDS BY MEANS OF WORDS
SPOKEN OUTWARDLY

For do teachers profess that it is their thoughts which are
perceived and grasped by the students, and not the sciences
themselves which they convey through speaking? For who is
so stupidly curious as to send his son to school in order that
he may learn what the teacher thinks? But all those sciences
which they profess to teach, and the science of virtue itself
and wisdom, teachers explain through words. Then those who
are called pupils consider within themselves whether what
has been explained has been said truly; looking of course to
that interior truth, according to the measure of which each is
able. Thus they learn, and when the interior truth makes
known to them that true things have been said, they applaud,
but without knowing that instead of applauding teachers they
are applauding learners, if indeed their teachers know what
they are saying. But men are mistaken, so that they call those
teachers who are not, merely because for the most part there
is no delay between the time of speaking and the time of
cognition. And since after the speaker has reminded them,
the pupils quickly learn within, they think that they have
been taught outwardly by him who prompts them.

46. But we shall, God willing, inquire at some other time
about the utility of words, which if it is well considered is no
mean matter. For the present I have warned you that we
should not attribute more to words than is proper. So that
now we may not only believe but also begin to understand
that it has truly been written on divine authority that we

are not to call anyone on earth our master because there is only one Master of all who is in heaven.[16] But what *in heaven* means He Himself will advertise to us by means of men, through signs and outwardly, so that we may by turning inwardly to Him be made wise; whom to know and to love is the blessed life which, though all claim to seek it, few indeed may rejoice that they have found. But now pray tell me what you think about this long disquisition of mine. For if you know that what I have said is true, then had you been questioned about each statement you would have said that you did know it. You see, therefore, from whom you have learned these matters. Surely, not from me to whom you would have given the correct answer if questioned. However, if you do not know that they are true, neither the inner man nor I have taught you; not I, because I can never teach; not the inner man, because you have it not yet in you to learn.

Ad.—But I have learned through being reminded by your words that man is only prompted by words in order that he may learn, and it is apparent that only a very small measure of what a speaker thinks is expressed in his words. Moreover, when He spoke among the people He reminded us that we learn whether things are true from that one only whose habitation is within us, whom now, by His grace, I shall so love more ardently as I progress in understanding. Nevertheless, I am most grateful to you for the discussion which you delivered without breaking the thread of your thought, because it anticipated and dissolved all the objections which occurred to me, and nothing which was causing me disquietude has been overlooked by you, nor is there anything about which the inner oracle does not tell me what your words stated.

[16] Matthew, XXIII, 8–10.

ON THE IMMORTALITY OF THE SOUL

(De immortalitate animae)

ONE BOOK

(Written about 387 A. D.)

CHAPTER I

THE FIRST REASON WHY THE SOUL IS IMMORTAL: IT IS THE SUBJECT
OF SCIENCE WHICH IS ETERNAL

1. If science [*disciplina*] exists anywhere, and cannot exist
except in that which lives; and if it is eternal, and nothing in
which an eternal thing exists can be non-eternal; then that
in which science exists lives eternally. If we exist who reason,
that is, if our mind does, and if our mind cannot reason rightly
without science, and if without science no mind can exist
except as a mind without science, then science is in the mind
of man. Science, moreover, is somewhere, for it exists, and
whatever exists cannot be nowhere. Further, science cannot
exist except in that which lives. For nothing which is not
alive learns anything, and science cannot be in a thing which
does not learn.

Again, science is eternal. For what exists and is unchangeable must be eternal. But no one denies that science exists.
And whoever admits that it is impossible that a line drawn
through the midpoint of a circle is not greater than all lines
which are not drawn through the midpoint, and admits that
this is a part of science, does not deny that science is unchangeable. Further, nothing in which an eternal thing exists
can be non-eternal. For nothing which is eternal ever allows
to be taken from it that in which it exists eternally.

Now, truly, when we reason it is the mind which reasons.

For only he who thinks reasons. Neither does the body think, nor does the mind receive the help of the body in thinking, since when the mind wishes to think it turns away from the body. For what is thought is thus eternal, and nothing pertaining to the body is thus eternal, therefore the body cannot help the mind as it strives to understand; for it is sufficient if the body does not hamper the mind. Again, without science [*disciplina*] nobody reasons rightly. For thought is right reasoning moving from things certain to the investigation of things uncertain, and there is nothing certain in an ignorant mind. All that the mind knows, moreover, it contains within itself, nor does knowledge consist in anything which does not pertain to some science. For science is the knowledge of any things whatsoever. Therefore the human mind always lives.

CHAPTER II

ANOTHER REASON: IT IS THE SUBJECT OF REASON WHICH IS NOT CHANGED

2. Surely, reason either is the mind or is in the mind. Our reason, moreover, is better than our body, and body is a substance, and it is better to be a substance than to be nothing. Therefore, reason is not nothing.

Again, whatever the harmony of the body is, it must be in the body inseparably as in a subject; and nothing may be held to be in the harmony unless it is also necessarily in that body inseparably as in a subject. But the human body is mutable and reason is immutable. For all which does not exist always in the same mode is mutable, but that two and two are four exists always in the same mode, and also that four contains two and two exists always in the same mode, but two does not contain four, therefore two is not four. This sort of reasoning, then, is immutable. Therefore, reason is immutable.

Moreover, if the subject is changed, there is no way in which that which is in the subject remains unchanged. Hence, it follows that the mind is not a harmony of the body. Nor can death befall unchangeable things. Consequently, the mind always lives, and either the mind is reason itself or has reason in it inseparably.

CHAPTER III

MIND IS LIVING SUBSTANCE AND IMMUTABLE; AND IF IT IS IN
SOME MODE MUTABLE, IT DOES NOT ON THAT ACCOUNT BECOME
MORTAL

3. Some power [*virtus*] is constant, and all constancy is unchangeable, and all power can act, nor does it cease to be power when it acts. Further, all action is moved or moves. Therefore, not all which is moved, or surely not all which moves, is changeable. But all which is moved by another and does not move itself is a mortal thing. Nor is anything immutable which is mortal. Hence, certainly and without any disjunction, it is concluded that not all which moves is changed.

There is, moreover, no motion without substance, and any substance either is alive or is not alive, and all which does not live is inanimate. But no action is inanimate. Therefore, that which moves so as not to be changed can be only living substance. Any action, moreover, moves the body through a number of steps; therefore, not all which moves the body is changeable. The body, moreover, is not moved except in time; and to the body pertains being moved faster and slower; therefore, there is shown to be a certain thing which moves in time and is not changed. Moreover, every body which moves in time, although it tends towards one end, yet can neither accomplish simultaneously all the steps which lead to this end, nor can avoid the several steps. For by whatever impulse it is moved, a body cannot be perfectly one, because it can be divided into parts; and there is no body without parts, as there is no time without an interval of delay, even if it is expressed by a very short syllable of which you hear neither the beginning nor the end. Further, what occurs thus needs expectation that it may be accomplished and memory that it may be understood as much as possible. And expectation is of future things, while memory is of things past. But intention to act belongs to present time, through which the future moves into the past. And without memory we cannot expect the end of a motion which has begun. For how can that be expected to cease which forgets either that it has begun or that it is in motion? Again, the intention of accomplishing which is present cannot be without expectation of the end which is future: nor does anything exist which does not yet exist or which has already ceased to exist. Therefore, there can be something in acting which pertains to those things which do not yet exist. There can be several things simultaneously in the agent, although these several acts when executed cannot exist simultaneously. Likewise, they can exist simultaneously in the mover, although they cannot in the thing moved. But whatever things cannot exist simultaneously in time, and yet are transmitted from future into past, must of necessity be mutable.

4. From the above we have already gathered that there can be a certain thing which is not changed when it moves changeable things. For when the intention of the mover to bring

the body which it moves to the end it desires is not changed, while the body which is acted upon is changed by this motion from moment to moment, and when that intention of accomplishment, which obviously remains unchanged, moves both the members of the artificer and the wood or stone which are subject to the artificer, who may doubt that what we have said follows as a logical consequence? Therefore, if any change in bodies be effected by the mind as mover, however intent upon the change the mind may be, we should not think that the mind is changed necessarily by this, or that the mind dies. For along with this intention it can have memory of past things and expectation of future things, none of which can exist without life. And even if there be no destruction without change, and no change without motion, yet not all change is engaged in destruction, nor is all motion engaged in change. For we can say that this body of ours has been for the most part moved by an action, and that it has undoubtedly been changed especially by age; still it has not yet perished, that is, is not without life. Therefore, from this it follows immediately that the mind is not deprived of life, even though some change does perchance occur to it through motion.

CHAPTER IV

ART AND THE UNCHANGEABLE PRINCIPLE OF NUMBERS, WHICH DO NOT INHERE IN THE MIND WITHOUT LIFE

5. For if there persists anything in the mind unchangeable, which cannot exist without life, then life must also remain in the mind eternally. For indeed the mind is so constituted that if the antecedent is true, the consequent is true. Moreover, the antecedent is true. For who dares say, not to men-

tion other things, either that the principle [*ratio*] of number is changeable or that there is any art which does not depend upon this principle [*ratio*]; or that an art is not in the artist even if he be not applying it; or that it is in him other than as being in the mind; or that it can be where there is no life; or that what is unchangeable cannot be anywhere; or that art is other than a principle [*ratio*]? For although an art is said to be a sort of assemblage of many principles [*rationes*], yet an art can in truth be called one principle [*ratio*] and can be so thought. But whether it be the former or the latter, it follows none the less that art is unchangeable. Moreover, it is clear not only that an art is in the mind of the artist, but also that it is nowhere else except in the mind, and in it inseparably. For if art is separated from the mind it will be other than in the mind, or will be nowhere, or will pass immediately from the mind. But just as there is no seat of art without life, so there is no life according to a principle [*ratio*] anywhere except in the soul. Further, that which is cannot be nowhere nor can that which is immutable be non-existent at any time. But if art passes from mind to mind, it would leave one mind and abide in another; in this case nobody would teach an art except by losing it, or further, nobody would become skilled except through the forgetting of his teacher, or by the teacher's death. If these things are utterly absurd and false, as they are, then the human mind is immortal.

6. And if indeed art exists at some time, it does not so exist in a mind which is conspicuous for its forgetfulness and ignorance. The conclusion of this argument adds nothing to the mind's immortality unless the preceding be denied in the following way. Either there is something in the mind which is not in present thought or else the art of music is not in the educated mind when it thinks of geometry alone. And

this latter is false. Hence the former is true. Moreover, the mind does not perceive that it contains anything except what comes into thought. Therefore, there can be something in the mind, which the mind itself does not perceive to be in it. But as long as it is there, this makes no difference. For if the mind has been occupied with other things too long to be able to turn its attention back to things thought of before, this is called forgetting or ignorance. But since, when we reason with ourselves or when we are skilfully questioned by another concerning certain liberal arts, we then discover the things which we discover nowhere else but in the mind; and since to discover is not to make or to cause, as otherwise the mind would cause eternal things through temporal discovery (for it often discovers eternal things, as the principle [ratio] of the circle, or anything else of this sort in the arts, which is not understood either to have been non-existent at some time or ever to be about to be); hence it is also evident that the human mind is immortal, and all true principles [rationes] are in its hidden places, although, either because of ignorance or forgetting, it seems not to contain them or to have lost them.

CHAPTER V

MIND IS NOT CHANGED SO THAT IT CEASES TO BE MIND

7. But now let us see to what extent we should accept the statement that the mind changes. For if the mind is the subject, with art existing in the subject, and if a subject cannot be changed unless that which is in it as in a subject be changed also, who can hold that art and principle [ratio] are unchangeable in the mind if the mind in which they exist is shown to be changeable? Moreover, where is there greater change than

that in contraries? And who denies that the mind is, to say the least, at times stupid and at other times wise? Therefore, let us see in how many ways that which is called change of the soul may be taken. Of these I think there are found two genera quite evident or at last quite clear to us, though there are found several species. For the soul is said to be changed either according to passions of the body or according to its own passions. According to the passions of the body, as through age, disease, sorrow, work, hatred, or carnal desires; according to its own passions, however, as by desiring, enjoying, fearing, worrying, striving, or learning.

8. All these changes, if they are not necessarily proof that the soul dies, ought not to be feared at all taken separately each by each; but it should be seen whether they oppose our reasoning in which we said that when a subject is changed all which is in the subject is necessarily changed. But they do not oppose it. For this is said of a subject according to such a change as makes the name change entirely. For if wax changes to a black color from white, it is none the less wax; and also if it assumes a round shape after being square, becomes hard when it has been soft, cools after being hot. These are all in the subject, and wax is the subject. But wax remains not more or less wax when these things are changed. Therefore, some change of the things in the subject can occur, when the subject itself is not changed with regard to what it is and is called. But if so much change occurs in those things which are in the subject that that which was said to be the subject cannot any longer be so called, as, for example, when from the heat of fire wax disappears into the air, and suffers such change that it may rightly be understood that the subject is changed, since it was wax, and is no longer wax; then by no reasoning of any kind whatever would we think that any of

those things would remain, which were in that subject because it was what it was.

9. Consequently, if, as we said above, the soul is a subject in which reason is inseparably (by that necessity also by which it is shown to be in the subject), neither can there be any soul except a living soul, nor can reason be in a soul without life, and reason is immortal; hence, the soul is immortal. For in absolutely no way could the soul remain immutable if its subject did not exist. This would happen if so great a change should befall the soul as would make it not a soul, that is, would compel it to die. Moreover, not one of those changes which occur to the soul, either through the body or through itself (although there is not a little question whether any occur through itself, that is, of which it is itself the cause), causes the soul not to be a soul. Therefore, they need not be feared *per se;* nor because they may oppose our reasoning.

CHAPTER VI

UNCHANGEABLE REASON, WHETHER IT BE IN THE MIND OR WITH
THE MIND, OR WHETHER THE MIND BE IN IT, CANNOT
BE SEPARATED FROM THE VERY SAME MIND

10. Hence I see that all men of reason ought to take pains to know what reason is and in how many ways it can be defined, so that it may remain firm according to all modes and with regard to the immortality of the soul. Reason is the aspect of the mind which perceives the true *per se* and not through the body; or it is the contemplation of the true, not through the body; or it is the true itself which is contem-

plated. Nobody doubts that the first of these is in the mind. There can be a question about the second and third; but even the second cannot exist without the mind. Concerning the third the great question is whether the true which is perceived by the mind without the instrument of the body exists *per se*, and is not in the mind, or whether it can exist without the mind. Moreover, in whatever mode the true may be, the mind cannot contemplate it *per se* except through some connection with it. For all that we contemplate we either perceive through cogitation [*cogitatio*], or through a sense or through the intellect. But those things which are perceived through sense we also sense to be outside us, and to be contained in places apart from which it is established that they cannot be perceived. But those things which are thought are not thought as being in another place other than the very mind which thinks them: for at the same time they also are thought as not being contained in any place.

11. Consequently, the connection between the mind which perceives and the true which it perceives is either such that the mind is the subject with the true in it as in a subject; or on the other hand the true is the subject with the mind in it as in a subject; or else each is a substance. Moreover, if the connection is of the first sort, the mind is as immortal as reason, according to the preceding argument, since reason can be in nothing but a living thing. The same necessity lies in the second sort of connection. For if the true, which is called reason, contains nothing which is changeable, as it appears, then nothing can be changed which is in it as in a subject. Therefore, all the struggle is left to the third. For if mind is one substance and reason another substance to which it is joined, he is not absurd who would think it possible for the former to remain while the latter perishes. But it is evident that as long as the mind is not separated from reason and remains connected with it, the mind necessarily survives and lives. But by what force can it be separated? By bodily force, whose power is weaker, whose origin is inferior, whose order is more disparate? Not at all. Then by animate strength? But how so? Cannot a more powerful mind contemplate reason without separating another mind from it? Reason is not lacking in any mind which contemplates, if all minds contemplate; and since nothing is more powerful than reason itself, than which nothing is more immutable, by no means will there be a mind not joined to reason and yet more powerful than one which is so joined. It remains that either reason separates itself from mind, or else the mind itself is separated by will. But there is no envy in that nature, and, therefore, it offers itself for mind's enjoyment; and, what is more, whatever it joins to itself it causes to be, which is contrary to destruction. Moreover, it is too absurd for someone to say that the mind is separated from reason by the mind's own will, provided there can be any mutual separation of things which space does not contain. Indeed this can be said in contradiction to all we have argued above in meeting other opposition. What then? Should it be concluded that the mind is immortal? Or, even though it cannot be separated, can it perhaps be extinguished? But if the very strength of reason affects the mind by its connection (and it cannot fail to affect it), then it at once causes being to be ascribed to mind. For it is in great measure reason itself in which the supreme immutability is thought. Therefore, that which reason affects by virtue of itself it causes to exist in a certain respect. Hence the mind cannot be extinguished unless it be separated from reason, and it cannot be separated, as we have proved above. Therefore it cannot perish.

CHAPTER VII

AND IF THE MIND TENDS THROUGH SUBSTANCE TOWARDS DEFECTION,
STILL IT DOES NOT ON THIS ACCOUNT PERISH

12. But that very turning away from reason by which
stupidity enters the mind cannot occur without a defect in
the mind. For if the mind has more being when turned towards
reason and inhering in it, thus adhering to the unchangeable
thing which is truth, both greatest and first; so when turned
away from reason it has less being, which constitutes a defection. Moreover, every defect tends towards nothing [non-
being], nor do we ever speak more properly of destruction
than when that which was something becomes nothing. Therefore, to tend towards nothing [non-being] is to tend towards
destruction. It is hard to say why this does not occur to the
soul in which defect occurs. We grant all the above, but we
deny that it follows that what tends towards nothing [non-
being] perishes, that is, that it reaches nothing. This can be
observed in the body also. For any body is part of the sensible
world, and for this reason the larger it is and the more space
it occupies the nearer it is to the universe; and the more it
does this, the greater it is. For the whole is greater than the
part. Hence, necessarily, it is less when it is diminished; that
is, it suffers a defect when it is lessened. Moreover, it is lessened when something is taken from it by cutting away, and
it follows from this that because of such subtraction it tends
to nothing. But no cutting away leads to nothing as such. For
every part which remains is a body, and whatever is a body
occupies a place in some space. Nor would this be possible
unless it were to have parts into which it might be cut again

and again. Therefore, it can be infinitely diminished through infinite division, and hence can suffer defection and tend towards nothing, although it can never reach nothing. Further, this can be said and understood of space itself and of any interval whatever. For by taking, let us say, a half part from the limits, and always a half part from what is left, the interval is diminished and approaches a limit which yet it can in no mode attain. Accordingly, even less should it be feared that the mind may become nothing, for the mind is indeed better and more lively than the body.

CHAPTER VIII

JUST AS THAT CANNOT BE TAKEN FROM BODY BY WHICH IT IS BODY, SO NEITHER CAN THAT BE TAKEN FROM MIND BY WHICH IT IS MIND

13. But if that which causes the body to be is not in the matter of the body but in the form, (which point is established by quite irrefutable reasoning, for a body is greater according as it has better form and is more excellent, and it is less according as it is uglier and is more deformed, which defect occurs not from a taking away of matter, about which enough has been said, but from a privation of form), then this should be questioned and discussed, lest someone assert that mind perishes through defect of form; for seeing that when it is stupid mind is deprived of some of its form, it may be believed that this privation can be increased so much as to deprive the mind of form in every mode, by this misfortune reducing it to nothing and causing it to perish. Hence, if we can succeed in showing that not even the body can be deprived of that by virtue of which it is body, perhaps we shall rightly maintain that the mind can much less have that taken from it by virtue of which it is mind. For whoever considers carefully will admit that any kind of mind whatever must be preferred to every body.

14. Let this, then, be the beginning of our argument, namely, that no thing makes or begets itself, unless it was before it existed: if the latter is false, the former is true. Again, that which has not been made or begotten, and yet is, must be everlasting. Whoever attributes this nature and this excellence to any body, errs indeed greatly. But why do we dispute? For even were we to attribute it to body we should be forced to attribute it much more to the mind. Thus if any body is everlasting, there is no mind which is not everlasting; seeing that any mind is to be preferred to any body and eternal things to non-eternal things. But if it is truly said that the body is made, it was made by some maker, nor was the maker inferior to body. For an inferior maker would not have power to give to that which he was making whatever it is that makes it what it is. But the maker and the body are not equals, since it is necessary for a maker to have something better for making than that which he makes. For we do not make the absurd statement that the begetter is that thing which is begotten by him. Therefore, a whole body has been made by some force which is more powerful and better, or at least not corporeal. For if a body be made by a body, it cannot be made whole; for it is very true, as we stated in the beginning of this argument, that no thing can be made by itself. Moreover, this force or incorporeal nature being the producer of the whole body preserves the whole by its abiding power. For it did not make a thing and then vanish and desert the thing made. Indeed that substance which is not body is not, if I may speak thus, moved in space so that it can be separated from that substance which is localized; and this effecting strength cannot be idle, but preserves that which it has made, and does not allow it to lack the form by virtue of which it is to whatever extent it is. For since the thing made does not exist *per se,* if it is abandoned by that through which it exists, it will immediately cease to exist, and we cannot say that when the body was made it received the power to be sufficient by virtue of itself when it is deserted by its maker.

15. And if this is so, the mind which clearly excels the body has power to a greater degree. And thus the mind is proved immortal, if it can exist *per se.* For whatever exists thus must be incorruptible, and therefore unable to perish, since nothing abandons itself. But the changeability of the body is manifest, which the whole motion of the entire body indicates adequately. Hence, it is found by those who investigate carefully, in so far as such a nature can be investigated, that ordered changeableness imitates that which is unchangeable. Moreover, that which exists *per se* has no need of anything, not even of motion, since it has all it needs existing in itself; for all motion is towards another thing which is that which is lacked by that which is moved. Therefore, form is present in the whole body while a better nature which made it provides for and sustains it, hence, that changeability does not take away from a body its being a body, but causes it to pass from one form to another by a well-ordered motion. For not one of its parts is allowed to be reduced to nothing, since that effective power with its force, neither striving nor inactive, aims at a whole, permitting the body to be all which through the power it is, in so far as it is. Consequently, there should be no one so devoid of reason as not to be certain that the mind is better than the body, or when this has been granted, to think that it does not happen to the body that the body is not body, yet happens to the mind that it is not mind. If this does not happen, and a mind cannot exist unless it lives, surely a mind can never die.

CHAPTER IX

MIND IS LIFE, AND THUS IT CANNOT LACK LIFE

16. If anyone asserts that the mind ought not to fear that destruction in which that which was something becomes nothing, but ought to fear that in which we call those things dead which lack life, let him notice that there is no thing which lacks itself. Moreover, mind is a certain life, so that all which is animated lives. But every inanimate thing which can be animated is understood to be dead, that is, deprived of life. Hence the mind cannot die. For if anything can lack life, this thing is not mind which animates, but a thing which has been animated. If this is absurd, this kind of destruction should be feared much less by the mind, since destruction of life is surely not to be feared. For if the mind dies wholly when life abandons it, that very life which deserts it is understood much better as mind, as now mind is not something deserted by life, but the very life itself which deserted. For whatever dead thing is said to be abandoned by life, is understood to be deserted by the soul. Moreover, this life which deserts the things which die is itself the mind, and it does not abandon itself; hence the mind does not die.

CHAPTER X

MIND IS NOT THE ORGANIZATION OF BODY

17. Unless perhaps we ought to believe that life is some organization [*temperatio*] of the body, as some have held. It would never have seemed so to them if they had been able to see those things which exist truly and which remain unchangeable when the same mind has been freed from the habit of bodies and cleansed. For who has looked well within himself without having experienced that the more earnestly he had thought something, the more he was able to move and draw the attention of the mind away from the senses of the body? If the mind were an organization of the body, this would absolutely not happen. For a thing which did not have a nature of its own and was not a substance, but which like color and shape was in the body inseparably as in a subject, would not try in any way to turn itself away from that same body in order to perceive intelligible things; and only inasmuch as it could do this would it be able to look upon intelligible things and be made by this vision better and more excellent. Indeed, in no way can shape or color, or the very organization of the body, which is a certain mixture of four natures in which the same body consists, turn from the thing in which they are inseparably as in a subject. In comparison with these things, those things which the mind thinks when it turns away from the body are not wholly corporeal, and yet they exist, and that in great degree, for they maintain themselves always in the same mode. For nothing more absurd can be said than that those things which we see with the eyes exist, while those things which we perceive by the intellect do not; for it is mad to doubt that the intellect is incomparably superior to the eyes. Moreover, while these things which are thought maintain themselves in the same mode, when the mind sees them it shows well enough that it is joined to them in a certain miraculous and likewise incorporeal way, that is, not locally. For either they are in it, or it is in them. And whichever one of these is true, either the one is in the other as in a subject, or each one is a substance. But if the first is true, the mind is not in the body as in a subject, as color and shape are, since either it is substance itself or it is in another substance which is not body. Moreover, if the second is true, mind is not in body as in a subject, as color is in body, because the mind is a substance. Further, the organization of a body is in the body as in a subject, just as color is; therefore, mind is not the organization of the body, but the mind is life. No thing deserts itself, and that dies which is deserted by life. Therefore, the mind cannot die.

CHAPTER XI

EVEN THOUGH TRUTH IS THE CAUSE OF THE MIND,
MIND DOES NOT PERISH THROUGH FALSEHOOD,
THE CONTRARY OF TRUTH

18. And so again, if anything should be feared, it is that the mind may perish by defection, that is, may be deprived of the very form of existence. Although I think enough has been said about this, and it has been shown by clear reasoning that this cannot be done, yet it should also be observed that there is no other reason for this fear except that we have admitted that the stupid mind exists defectively, while the wise mind exists in more certain and fuller essence. But if, as nobody doubts, the mind is most wise when it looks upon truth which is always in the same mode, and clings immovable to it, joined by divine love; and if all things which exist in any mode whatever exist by that essence which exists in the highest and greatest degree; then either the mind exists by virtue of that essence, inasmuch as it does exist, or it exists *per se*. But if it exists *per se,* since it is itself the cause of its existing and never deserts itself, it never perishes, as we also argued above. But if we exist from that essence there is need to inquire carefully what thing can be contrary to it, which may rob the mind of being the mind which the essence causes. So, then, what is it? Falsity, perhaps, because the essence is truth? But it is manifest and clearly established to what extent falsity can harm the mind. For can it do more than deceive? And except he live is any deceived? Therefore, falsity cannot destroy the mind. But if what is contrary to truth cannot rob the mind of that being mind which truth gave it (for truth is thus unconquerable), what else may be found which may take from the mind that which is mind? Nothing, surely; for nothing is more able than a contrary to take away that which is made by its contrary.

CHAPTER XII

THERE IS NO CONTRARY TO THE TRUTH BY WHICH
MIND EXISTS IN SO FAR AS IT EXISTS

19. But suppose we seek the contrary of truth, not inasmuch as it is truth as the contrary of falsity, but inasmuch as it exists in the greatest and highest degree (although truth exists thus to the extent that it is truth, if we call that truth by which all things are true, in whatever degree they may exist, they exist inasmuch as they are true); yet by no means shall I seek to avoid that which this suggests to me so clearly. For if there is no contrary to any essence inasmuch as it is an essence, then much less is there a contrary to that first essence inasmuch as it is essence. Moreover, the antecedent is true. For no essence exists for any other reason than that it exists. Being, moreover, has no contrary except non-being: hence nothing is the contrary of essence. Therefore, in no way can anything exist as a contrary to that substance which exists first and in highest degree. If the mind has its very essence from that essence (for since it does not have it from itself [*ex se*] it cannot have it otherwise than from that thing which is superior to the mind itself); then there is no thing by which it may lose its existence (being), because there is nothing contrary to that thing from which it has it. Hence the mind cannot cease to exist. But since the mind has wisdom because of turning to that by virtue of which it exists, so also when it turns away it can lose this wisdom. For turning away is the contrary of turning toward. But what it has from that to which there is no contrary is not a thing which it can lose. Therefore, it cannot perish.

CHAPTER XIII

NOR IS MIND CHANGED INTO BODY

20. Here perhaps some question may appear as to whether the mind which does not perish is not changed into a lower essence. For it can appear to some, and not unjustly, that this reasoning proves that the mind cannot reach nothing, yet can be perhaps changed into body. For if what was formerly mind becomes body it will not yet be wholly non-existent. But this is impossible unless the mind desires it or else is compelled by another. Yet mind will not necessarily be able to be body, even if it desires it, or if it is compelled. For if it is body it follows that it desires this or is compelled. But it does not follow that if it desires or is compelled, it is body. Moreover, it will never desire to be body: for all the mind desires in regard to body is that it may possess it, or make it live, or fashion it in a certain manner, or look out for it in some way or other. Moreover, none of these things is possible if mind is not better than body. But if mind is body, it follows that it will not be better than body. Therefore, it will not wish to be body. Nor is there

any surer proof of this than when the mind questions itself about this point. For thus the mind easily discovers that it has no desire except for some action, either knowing or sensing, or only living to the fullest extent of its power.

21. But if it is compelled to be body, by what, pray, is it compelled? Whatever it is it must surely be more powerful than mind, hence it cannot be compelled by body itself; for no body can in any way be more powerful than mind. Moreover, a more powerful mind compels only that which is set under its power, and no mind can in any way be set under the power of another mind except by the former's own desire. Hence, one mind does not compel another mind more than the desires of the other allow. Moreover, it has been said that mind cannot have desire to be body. Also it is clear that the mind attains no satisfaction of its desire while it loses all desire, which happens when it is made body. Therefore, a mind cannot be compelled to become body by one whose only right to compel lies in the desires of the one compelled. Then whatever mind has another mind in its power must prefer having it to having a body in its power, and must wish to promote its goodness or to have power over evil. Therefore, it will not wish it to be body.

22. Finally, the mind which compels either is animal or it lacks body. But if it lacks body it is not in this world. And if it is thus, it is supremely good and cannot wish another to suffer such a wicked change. But if it is animal, either the mind it compels is animal or it is not. But if it is not, it cannot be compelled to anything by another. For none is more powerful than that which exists in the greatest degree. On the other hand, if it is body, again it is forced through body to whatever extent it is forced. But who believes that in any way such a change can be made in mind through body? For it would be made if the body were greater than it; although no matter what it is to which it is compelled by body it is not compelled wholly through body, but is compelled through its own desires, about which enough has been said. Moreover, that which is better than a rational soul is God, as all agree. He surely looks after the soul, and, therefore, the soul cannot be forced by Him to be changed into body.

CHAPTER XIV

NOR IS THE STRENGTH OF THE MIND DIMINISHED BY
SLEEP OR ANY OTHER SIMILAR AFFECTION OF
THE BODY

23. Hence, if the mind does not suffer this change by its own will, or because it is compelled by another, by what means can it suffer it? Or, because sleep for the most part overtakes us against our will, should it be feared that by some such defect the mind may be changed to body? As if when our limbs are overwhelmed by sleep to say that the mind is made weaker in some sense. Sensible things only it does not sense, because whatever causes sleep pertains to the body and works in the body. Sleep lulls and shuts off the corporeal senses so soundly that the soul submits with pleasure to such a change of the body. Such a change is according to nature and refreshes the body after its labors, yet it does not take from the mind the power of sensing and thinking. For it still has images of sensible things at hand of such evident similarity that at the time they cannot be distinguished from the things of which they are the images. If the mind thinks anything, it is as true in sleeping as in waking. For, to give an example, if it should argue to itself in a dream, and following true principles in argument should learn something, when it is awakened the same principles remain immutable, although other things may be found

false, such as the place where the argument seemed to have occurred, the person with whom it seemed to have been held,
even, as far as sound is concerned, the words themselves by
which it seemed the argument was made, and other things of
this sort. Likewise when these things are perceived and discussed by those who are awake, they pass away and in no sense
attain the eternal presence of true principles. From this it is
inferred that when a body changes as in sleep the soul's use of
that body can be diminished, but not its own life.

CHAPTER XV

AGAIN, MIND CANNOT BE CHANGED INTO BODY

24. Finally, however much the soul is joined to a body oc-
cupying space, still it is not joined locally. The soul is prior to
the body in connection with those supreme and eternal principles which survive unchangeably and are not contained in
space; and the soul's connection is not only prior but also
greater; as much prior as it is nearer, and for the same reason
as much greater as it is better than body. And this nearness
is not in place but in the order of nature. According to this
order it is understood that the supreme essence bestows form
upon the body through the soul by which it exists in whatever
degree it does exist. Therefore, the body subsists through the
soul, and it exists to the extent that it is animated, whether
universally, as the world, or particularly, as some animal or
other within the world. Therefore, the conclusion was that a
soul would become body through a soul, or else not at all. Since
it does not become body, and the soul remains soul in that in
which it is the soul, the body subsists through the soul which
gives it form and does not take this form away; hence the soul

cannot be changed into body. For if it does not give up the form which it takes from the Supreme Good, it does not become body through that form; and if it does not become body through that, either it does not become body at all, or else takes a form as near the Supreme Good as soul. But if, when it became body, it assumed a form as near the Supreme Good as soul, that form would be a soul; for this is important, that the soul is better to the extent to which it takes a form nearer the Supreme Good. Moreover, body would take a form of the corporeal order even if it did not take its form through soul. For if nothing intervened it would still take a form in this order. Nor is there found anything which exists between the Supreme Life which is wisdom and truth unchangeable and that remote thing which is made alive (that is, body), except the soul which makes the body live. If the soul gives form to body, so that body may exist to the extent that it does exist, it does not take the form away by giving. Moreover, it takes the soul into the body by transmutation. Therefore, the soul does not become body, either *per se,* because body is not made by soul unless the soul remains, or through another, because not except by giving form is body made through soul, and by taking away form soul would be changed into body, if it were changed.

CHAPTER XVI

NOR EVEN IS THE RATIONAL SOUL CHANGED INTO THE
IRRATIONAL. THE WHOLE SOUL IS IN THE BODY
AS A WHOLE AND IN EACH PART

25. Likewise it can be said that the rational soul is not changed into the irrational soul or life. For the irrational soul, even were it not held in a lower order by the rational soul,

would nevertheless assume the same form it does assume and be moved as it is. Therefore, more powerful things receive form from the Supreme Excellence and give it to things in the natural order. And when they give, surely, they do not take away. And to whatever extent the things which are inferior exist, they exist because the form in which they exist is given to them by those more powerful than they. And, indeed, the more powerful are also better. For to these natures it has been granted, not that through greater mass they have more power over things of lesser mass, but that without any increase of local magnitude they are more powerful than and better than the lower forms. In this way the soul is better than and greater than the body. Therefore, since the body, as has been said, subsists through the soul, the soul can in no way be changed into body; for no body is made except by receiving its form from the soul. The soul, if it became body, would become body through losing form, not through receiving it; therefore, it is not possible, unless perhaps the soul be contained in a place and joined locally to the body. For if this were true, although the soul is more perfect in form, perhaps a greater mass could change the soul into its lower form, just as the greater air changes the lesser fire. But it is not true. Indeed, every mass which occupies a place is not a separate whole in each of its parts, but the whole consists of all the parts. Consequently, one part of such a whole is in one place, and another in another. But the soul is present as a whole not only in the entire mass of a body, but also in every least part of the body at the same time. For the soul senses the suffering of a part of the body as a whole, and yet not in the whole body. For when there is a pain in the foot the eye turns, the tongue speaks, the hand moves forward. This would not happen unless the soul which senses in these parts, also senses in the foot, nor could it while absent sense what was happening there. For it is not to be believed that it happens through any agent of communication which does not sense what it communicates; for the suffering which occurs does not run through the whole extent of the mass in such a way as to involve all the other parts of the soul which are elsewhere. Rather, the whole soul senses what happens to the foot in particular, and only senses it at the place at which it happens. The whole soul, therefore, is present simultaneously in each part, and simultaneously senses in each. Yet the soul is not wholly present in the way in which whiteness or any other quality of this sort is wholly present in each part of a body. For what a body suffers in one part by change of whiteness cannot pertain to the whiteness which is in another part. Hence, it is shown that a mass itself is differentiated according as its parts are differentiated. But we have proved above that this is not the case with the soul as it senses.

(Order of works as given by L'Abbé Jules Martin on page 397 of his *Saint Augustin*.)

Roman Empire in the West,
Constantius II, 337–361

St. Augustine born at Tagaste, in Numidia, Nov. 13	354
St. Augustine becomes a Manichee (age 19)	373
Lectures on rhetoric at Carthage and Tagaste	
De pulchro et apto. (?)	
St. Augustine goes to Rome to teach rhetoric	383
Contra academicos, Lib. II	386
De beata vita ⎱ (Platonic and	
De ordine, Lib. II ⎰ Neo platonic influence)	
St. Augustine, Professor of Eloquence at Milan	
(Pauline Epistles), Ambrose, Bishop of Milan	
St. Augustine baptized at Milan, Easter, April 25	387
(age 33)	
Soliloquiorum, Lib. II	
De immortalitate animae	
De musica, Lib. VI	388
De quantitate animae	
St. Augustine departs for Africa	
De moribus ecclesiae et Manichaeorum, Lib. II	
St. Augustine ordained priest by Valerius, Bishop of Hippo	
De diversis quaestionibus, LXXXIII	
De libero arbitrio, Lib. III	
De magistro	389
De genesi contra Manichaeos, Lib. II	
De vera religione	390
De utilitate credendi	391
De duabus animabus	

85

392–395, Theodosius I
(Emperor of the East)

476, Abolition of the Western Cæsar and Reunion to
the Eastern Empire in nominal suzerainty

Available Editions of the Works of St. Augustine

Opera omnia, opere et studio monachorum S. Benedicti.

Opera omnia, Patrologie Latine, Vols. 32–47. Librairie Garnier Frères, Paris. (Chaque volume se vend séparément.)

Corpus Scriptorum Ecclesiasticorum Latinorum, 13 vols. Vienna, 1908.

De doctrina christiana libros quattuor editit H. J. Vogels. 1930. VI. 103 p. Peter Hanstein Verlagsbuchhandlung, Bonn.

De beata vita liber. Editit M. Schmaus. 1931. As above.

Translations

The Nicene and Post-Nicene Fathers. (Theological works and controversies.) Christian Literature Co., 1887. (Edition out of print.) Charles Scribner's Sons. (Later: out of print.)

The Soliloquies, tr. by R. E. Cleveland. William and Norgate, London, 1910; Little, Brown and Company, Boston.

On Free Will, Book II. Vol. I, p. 3, of *Selections from Medieval Philosophers,* edited by Richard McKeon. Charles Scribner's Sons, New York.

Confessions, tr. by J. G. Pilkington. Boni and Liveright. Also Loeb Classical Library, Harvard University Press.

The City of God, an abridged edition. J. M. Dent and Sons, Ltd., London; E. P. Dutton and Co., New York.

Commentary

Introduction a L'Étude de SAINT AUGUSTIN, par Étienne Gilson. Librairie Philosophique J. Vrin, Paris, 1931.

La Philosophie de Saint Augustin, Nourrisson, 2 vols. Didier et Cie., 1865. (Historical sources.)

Saint Augustin, par L'Abbé Jules Martin, seconde édition. Librairie Felix Alcan, Paris, 1923.

Saint Augustin, Louis Bertrand. A. Fayard et Cie., 1913. (A biographical history.)
Saint Augustin et le Néo-platonisme, Grandgeorge.

In General

The Spirit of Mediæval Philosophy, Étienne Gilson. Charles Scribner's Sons, 1936, New York.
St. Thomas Aquinas's *De Magistro,* tr. by M. H. Mayer. Bruce Publishing Co., New York.
The Meaning of Meaning, Ogden and Richards. Harcourt, Brace and Company, New York.
Works of Plato, Preferably Loeb Library translations.
Reduction of the Arts to Theology, St. Bonaventura.
Enneades, Plotinus, texte établi et trad. p. E. Bréhier, vols. 1–6.

(1)

1.25

1/44